EAST PROVIDENCE PUBLIC LIBRARY
RIVERSIDE BRANCH

APR   1999

No Longer Property of
East Providence Public Library

W9-BBZ-787

EAST PROVIDENCE PUBLIC LIBRARY
RIVERSIDE BRANCH

CULTURES OF THE WORLD

HONDURAS

Leta McGaffey

MARSHALL CAVENDISH
New York • London • Sydney

EAST PROVIDENCE PUBLIC LIBRARY
    RIVERSIDE BRANCH

j910
cul

Reference edition published 1999 by
Marshall Cavendish Corporation
99 White Plains Road
Tarrytown
New York 10591

© Times Editions Pte Ltd 1999

MC 4/19/99 150L/6V

Originated and designed by
Times Books International, an imprint of
Times Editions Pte Ltd

All rights reserved. No part of this book may be reproduced or
utilized in any form or by any means electronic or mechanical,
including photocopying, recording, or by an information storage
and retrieval system, without permission from the copyright
owner.

Printed in Malaysia

Library of Congress Cataloging-in-Publication Data:

McGaffey, Leta.
    Honduras / Leta McGaffey.
        p. cm.—(Cultures of the World)
    Includes bibliographical references and index.
    ISBN 0-7614-0955-6 (library binding)
    1. Honduras—Juvenile literature. I. Title. II. Series.
F1503.2.M34   1999
972.83—dc21   98–54908
                    CIP
                    AC

3 1499 00287 4151

INTRODUCTION

HONDURAS IS A COUNTRY of friendly, happy, gracious people even though many Hondurans, both rural and urban, live in poverty. Hondurans live in a beautiful and diverse region with glorious mountains, sunny beaches, and dense, lush rainforests. The second largest country in Central America, Honduras remains a dominantly agricultural society. Although Honduras has been through many hardships since colonization by the Spanish, it has maintained a relatively peaceful political climate that other Central American countries have been unable to match.

The population of Honduras includes culturally strong indigenous groups, but most Hondurans today are a cultural mix of indigenous and Spanish peoples. The country is beginning to enjoy its relatively new reputation as a traveler's paradise because of its exotic beauty, wildlife diversity, and remoteness.

CONTENTS

A young Honduran girl carries her load in the traditional manner.

CONTENTS

Roosters figure in Honduran folklore and folk crafts.

GEOGRAPHY

THE REPUBLIC OF HONDURAS is a beautiful, mountainous country approximately the size of the state of Ohio or Pennsylvania, with an area of 43,277 square miles (112,087 square km). It is the second largest country in Central America, bordering on Guatemala in the west, El Salvador in the southwest, and Nicaragua in the southeast, with an extensive coastline of 457 miles (735 km) along the Caribbean Sea in the north. There is also a small gulf in the southwest off the Pacific Ocean, the Gulf of Fonseca, with a coastline of 90 miles (145 km). Honduras stretches between 13 and 16 degrees north of the equator and between 83 and 89 degrees longitude west.

Honduras is a country of natural diversity with rugged mountains, vast pine forests, idyllic beaches, flat savannas (treeless grassland), coral reefs, and acres of fertile banana fields.

Left: **A coastal village on the north or Caribbean shore of Honduras.**

Opposite: **A wildlife refuge on the south shore, off the Gulf of Fonseca.**

Río Patuca flows through the Patuca Mountains. Dense forests on slopes characterize a large part of the Honduran landscape.

TOPOGRAPHY AND GEOGRAPHICAL REGIONS

There are four distinct geographical regions on mainland Honduras as well as the unique Bay Islands off the north coast. Over two-thirds of Honduras consists of interior highlands with dramatic mountains and valleys. The Mosquito Coast, near the Nicaraguan border, is covered with dense rainforest. Along the Caribbean coast, there is a stretch of long, narrow lowlands where thousands of acres of banana plantations thrive. Just off the Gulf of Fonseca in the south, there is a smaller area of lowlands.

INTERIOR HIGHLANDS The most prominent feature of Honduran topography is the interior highlands made up of extinct volcanoes. Mountainous terrain makes up over 80% of the land. This is where most of the population lives, although the mountains are difficult to travel through and to cultivate.

A major mountain range, the Cordillera Merendón, runs from the southwest to the northeast. The highest peaks are found here, including

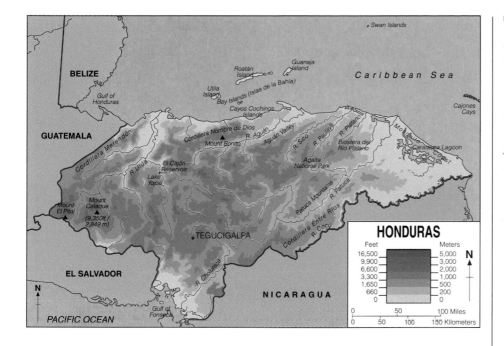

Although the Caribbean lowlands embrace only 15% of the land, it supports 25% of the population of Honduras.

the highest mountain, Mount Celaque (9,350 feet/2,849 m). The Cordillera Nombre de Dios range lies south of the Caribbean shore. It is not as rugged as the Merendón range but has peaks rising to 8,000 feet (2,440 m). The Cordillera Entre Ríos forms part of the border with Nicaragua.

Scattered throughout the interior highlands are numerous flat-floored valleys, 1,000–3,000 feet (300–900 m) in elevation. These fertile valleys support commercial agriculture and livestock. Subsistence farming has been relegated to the slopes of the valleys, while the large agribusinesses work the more arable, broad valley floors in an effort to increase the country's exports.

Villages and towns, including the capital, Tegucigalpa, have been built in the larger valleys. The Sula Valley is an extensive depression that runs from the Caribbean to the Pacific, providing a relatively convenient transportation route.

PACIFIC LOWLANDS The smallest geographical region of Honduras, the Pacific lowlands, is a strip of land only 15 miles (24 km) wide on the north shore of the Gulf of Fonseca. This fertile plain was formed from

Along the coast of the Gulf of Fonseca are salt-pans where seawater is collected and left in the sun for the water to evaporate, leaving behind salt for all of Honduras.

volcanic soil washing down from the mountains. Cattle ranches make use of the savannas. Mangroves along the shore provide breeding grounds for shrimp and shellfish. Two islands in the Gulf of Fonseca, El Tigre and Zacate Grande, have volcanic cones rising to over 2,200 feet (670 m).

CARIBBEAN LOWLANDS Hondurans refer to the Caribbean lowlands as "the north coast," or simply "the coast." This region has been by far the most exploited area, but development accelerated in the late 1800s when the banana industry flourished.

The central part of the lowlands is narrow: only a few miles wide. To the east and west of this section, however, it opens up into a wide coastal plain where banana plantations abound. The alluvial plains and coastal sierras produce rich crops of fruit and vegetables.

MOSQUITO COAST Indigenous people, including the Garifuna, Pech, and Miskito Indians, still inhabit this hot, humid region on the eastern Caribbean coast, which blends into mountain slopes. It is difficult to reach by road, and the most common forms of transportation is by airplane or boat. The dense rainforests of this region have been exploited to the

La Tigra National Park is a popular destination for day trippers from Tegucigalpa. It is a cloud forest preserve for a large variety of plant and animal life. The park's moss-covered world of trees laden with bromeliads, orchids, and ferns lends a feeling of mystery. The many mammals include tapirs, monkeys, and the rarely seen ocelot and jaguar. The park is also home to numerous colorful birds, including the resplendent quetzal, the emerald toucan, and the cinnamon-bellied flower-piercer. Visitors to La Tigra can hike miles of well-maintained, well-marked trails past a scenic waterfall and an abandoned silver mine or traverse the length of the park via a lookout point with an impressive view of Tegucigalpa.

danger point by logging. The Caratasca Lagoon—a large body of salt water connected to the Caribbean by a narrow inlet—is located here.

Except for the town of Amapala, the island of El Tigre in the Gulf of Fonseca has an air of isolation.

THE BAY ISLANDS together make the perfect tropical island paradise. They are lush emerald islands crowded with palm trees and surrounded by the turquoise Caribbean Sea. There are three large islands, Roatán, Utila, and Guanaja, three smaller islands, Helene, Morat, and Barbareta, as well as a biological reserve on the island of Cayos Cochinos. There are also more than 60 islets scattered in the area.

The Bay Islands are the tips of ancient underwater volcanoes. These islands have a diverse geography, ranging from densely jungled mountains to outstanding barrier reefs that attract divers and snorkelers from all over the world. The rainy season on the islands lasts from October to as late as February. March and August are the hottest months, but during the rest of the year, gentle sea breezes cool the air. Some of the islands are uninhabited, some have a few people living on them, and some are being developed for tourism.

The vivid underwater world of the barrier reef off Roatán Island draws divers from around the world.

Roatán is the largest, most populated, and most developed of the Bay Islands. It has a long, irregular mountain range inland with peaks that reach 770 feet (235 m). There are also hillside pastures, limestone caves, and clumps of lush green forest. White, sandy beaches and cliffs make up the north shore, while sandy inlets and bays punctuate the south shore. A beautiful, protected barrier reef circling the island draws many tourists. The people live along the coast, many in white clapboard, tin-roofed houses on stilts. There are a few culturally rich villages inhabited by friendly residents. These are located near historical sites that tell interesting tales of the first pirates to invade the Bay Islands. The economic hub of Roatán is French Harbor, home to the largest fishing fleet in this area of the Caribbean.

RIVERS

Rivers define half of Honduras' borders with El Salvador and Nicaragua. Numerous rivers drain the highlands during heavy rainfall and have carved out wide, fertile valleys, but there is only one natural lake, Lake Yojoa. The most important river is Río Ulúa, which flows northeast through the Sula Valley into the Gulf of Honduras. In some areas, such as the Biosfera del Río Plátano, river travel is the chief means of penetrating the region.

CLIMATE

The interior highlands have tropical wet and dry seasons. Almost all the rain falls during the wet season from May to September. Tegucigalpa,

HURRICANE MITCH

The most recent natural disaster to hit Honduras was the rampage of Hurricane Mitch in late October 1998. The rare Class Five hurricane with winds of up to 180 miles per hour (290 km/h) began its destruction of Honduras when it sat for two days over Guanaja, one of the Bay Islands, which was devastated. By the time it reached the mainland of Honduras, it was classified as a tropical storm. However, the amount of rain that was dumped onto almost every inch of Honduras (up to 4 feet/1 meter in many areas) created mud slides that literally buried whole villages, highways, and roads, and wiped out most bridges in the country. The cap of an extinct volcano fell off due to the rains and wiped out the villages in its path. Honduran cities and villages were left totally isolated except by air.

The storm killed an estimated 6,400 people in Honduras. A week after the storm had subsided, 11,000 were still missing and 600,000 people were left homeless and living in crowded shelters on high land. The hurricane wreaked havoc on the fertile Aguan and Sula valleys, destroying thousands of acres of banana and palm plantations. Approximately 70% of the nation's crops were destroyed—some fruit companies on the Caribbean coast lost 100% of their crops. Over 60% of the nation's infrastructure, including major bridges, were demolished. The total damage to infrastructure alone, not including loss in exports, was estimated at US$2 billion.

Amid the devastation, Hondurans counted their blessings. Roatán, one of the most developed areas of Honduras and a major tourist draw, was left relatively unscathed. The El Cajón Reservoir regained its optimal level, allowing the country's generators to work at full capacity without imported oil. Aid poured in from countries around the world to Honduras and other Central American countries that were badly damaged by the hurricane. Many countries wrote off debts owed to them by Honduras and its neighbors in an effort to help them rebuild their homelands.

One of the worst losses for residents of Tegucigalpa during Hurricane Mitch was that of their mayor. Dr. Cesar Castellanos was killed in a helicopter crash on All Saints' Day (November 1), 1998, when he was out surveying the damage to his beloved city. Residents are planning to rebuild the city with more hurricane-proof bridges and buildings, and to restrict construction on floodplains. They want to take this opportunity to build a cleaner, healthier capital that they can be proud of, partly in memory of Mayor Castellanos.

located in the highlands, has a pleasant climate ranging from 86°F (30°C) in April, the warmest month, to 77°F (25°C) in January, the coolest month. As elevation increases, temperature decreases. Above 6,000 feet (1,800 m) there is sometimes even frost after a cold night.

The Pacific lowlands also have wet and dry seasons with year-round high temperatures between 82°F (28°C) and 90°F (32°C). The dry season occurs between November and April, usually the hottest month of the year. During the rainy season the high humidity makes the heat uncomfortable.

Hiking in the cloud forest of Agalta National Park.

The Caribbean lowlands have a tropical wet climate with high temperatures and humidity and rainfall year round. These conditions have made the Caribbean lowlands ideal for growing bananas and pineapples, which need warm, wet weather. The only relief from the hot weather comes in December or January with high winds but only slightly cooler temperatures. The Caribbean coast is particularly prone to hurricanes and tropical storms, because Honduras lies within the hurricane belt. These storms usually travel inland from the Caribbean. Hurricanes occasionally form over the Pacific, but these are usually less severe, if they come over land at all.

FLORA

Honduras, like any tropical country, has a variety of vegetation that amazes people from temperate climates. Honduras' forests have only recently been set aside as national parks and biological reserves. On top of mountains and along ridges are cloud forests. These "weeping woods," as they are called, catch the moisture in the air, creating an ideal environment for ferns, vines, orchids, and broadleaf plants to grow. A rich humus of decaying matter covers the forest floor, and bromeliads flourish in the crooks of trees. Many varieties of wild avocado grow in abundance in varying moisture conditions.

Near these humid peaks are patches of desert deprived of moisture because the cloud forests catch all the water. At lower elevations pines and firs cover the mountainsides. In the savannas of the northeast are acacias and cacti, while in the warmer and wetter lowlands are mahogany, Spanish cedar, rosewood, palm trees, and mangroves. Besides avocadoes, tropical fruit that grow in abundance are tamarind, mango, pineapple, guava, papaya, and of course, bananas.

The graceful white-tailed deer is the national animal of Honduras.

FAUNA

Honduras' different ecological climates allow for a wide variety of mammals, fish, birds, amphibians, reptiles, and insects.

Honduras has many of the forest animals found in the United States, but also some exotic mammals. There are brocket deer, raccoons, coyotes, armadillos, foxes, squirrels, porcupines, monkeys, jaguars, and other large cats. There are also animals found only in tropical America, such as the kinkajou, a tree-dwelling mammal with brown fur and a prehensile tail, also called the honey bear.

Honduras is home to a wide variety of snakes including boa, worm, coral, bushmaster, rattlesnake, and fer-de-lance. There are also many species of brightly colored frogs and toads. In and near the water are

Above: **The national bird of Honduras, *la guaca-maya* ("gwah-kah-MAH-yah"), or the macaw.**

Right: **A biologist with an iguana he has captured.**

It takes an early riser to spot the elusive quetzal. Just after dawn these resplendent birds drop out of the trees in the cloud forest to eat a breakfast of blackberries.

crocodiles, caymans, manatees, and salamanders. Numerous turtles, such as the huge leatherback, live either in the sea or on the shore. Lizards are everywhere. Little hand-size geckos find a home anywhere, and iguanas can grow to 6 feet (1.8 m) long.

Lake Yojoa has large black bass that provide excellent game fishing. Sharks, catfish, barracuda, grouper, and mackerel are just a few examples of the ocean life found in the Caribbean Sea and the Gulf of Fonseca. There are mollusks such as snails, lobster, and freshwater crabs.

Over 700 species of birds are found in Honduras. Of note are swallows, green ibis, tiger heron, spotted wood-quails, cuckoos, macaws, quetzals, and a beautiful cloud forest trogon with iridescent red and green feathers and long tail feathers that arc like a peacock's.

There are many species of butterflies, moths, beetles, spiders, bees, wasps, ants, flies, and mosquitoes, many of them brightly colored.

CITIES AND TOWNS

Honduras is the only Latin American country that has the majority of its urban population distributed between two large centers: Tegucigalpa and San Pedro Sula. Although Honduras is still primarily an agrarian society, these two cities have grown considerably since the 1920s as Hondurans migrate from rural areas to find jobs. The cities contrast dramatically: Tegucigalpa is the political capital, whereas San Pedro Sula is the industrial and commercial center. Other cities in Honduras include La Ceiba, Copán, Santa Rosa de Copán, El Progreso, and the largest port, Puerto Cortés.

There are numerous towns in the western half of Honduras. Many of them are set amid splendid countryside and are places with interesting historical and native legends. Small towns like La Esperanza, Gracias, and Santa Lucía attract a steady stream of tourists.

TEGUCIGALPA The capital city of Honduras, Tegucigalpa is built into the hills of the central highlands. It was named the capital city in 1880.

Tegucigalpa got its name from two Indian words, *teguz* ("TEH-goos," or "hill") and *galpa* ("GAHL-pa," or "silver") because it was originally a small mining town.

The spectacular 328-foot (100 m) Pulhapanzák waterfalls near San Pedro Sula.

"Comayagüela" is Spanish for "little Comayagua." There is another town in Honduras with a similar name— Comayagua.

Tegucigalpa has the flavor of a small colonial city with brightly colored houses built into the hillsides and narrow, winding streets. At the center of the city are Spanish colonial churches, many government buildings, including the National Palace and the Presidential Palace, and numerous schools. This landmark historic center includes the Plaza Morazán, often called Parque Central, with a statue of the national hero Francisco Morazán. Overlooking Tegucigalpa is the United Nations National Park on Picacho Mountain. This park is recognized for its magnificent gardens of tropical plants and flowers, including beautiful Honduran orchids. Residents of Tegucigalpa flock to the park on Sundays, and use the outdoor grills for picnics.

Tegucigalpa experienced near-crippling population growth beginning in the 1950s when it increased by 75%. One million people live in Tegucigalpa and its sister city Comayagüela. Many of them today still have inadequate housing and either do not have running water or receive an inadequate supply.

SAN PEDRO SULA, the industrial capital of Honduras, is the bustling center of business transactions. It is located in the flat, fertile Sula Valley surrounded by banana plantations, and it has almost half a million residents. The population of this city is more multicultural than the rest of the country. The San Pedranos, as they call themselves, are friendly, outgoing, and helpful to foreign visitors.

San Pedro Sula was founded in 1536 as an agricultural town. Its importance increased speedily with the growth of the fruit companies on the north coast, and the city has become the center of agricultural business for the region. San Pedro Sula is considered possibly the fastest growing city in Central America.

The city has modern glass towers as well as residential areas where stately homes with green lawns offer an old-world charm and people stroll along tree-lined avenues in the evenings.

San Pedro Sula is extremely hot because it is only 250 feet (76 m) above sea level, with temperatures ranging from 80°F (27°C) to 100°F (38°C) year round.

San Pedro Sula has less evidence of poverty than Tegucigalpa and many other Honduran cities. It offers excellent restaurants, hotels, museums, and nightclubs.

Above: **A view of the Caribbean Sea from La Ceiba.**

Opposite: **Beyond Santa Lucía's tiled roofs is the landscape typical of the interior highlands, giving this town that lies just outside Tegucigalpa a secluded air.**

PUERTO CORTÉS, the largest and most important port in Honduras, is also the most modern port in Central America with large container facilities that stretch for 16 miles (5 km) along the bay. It is only a two-day sail from New Orleans or Miami. Puerto Cortés grew quickly in order to accommodate the export of bananas, and later as a center for oil refining. It also has numerous manufacturing companies that export products such as baseballs and luxury sailing boats.

LA CEIBA Nestled on the narrow coastal plain between the Cordillera Nombre de Dios and the Caribbean coast, La Ceiba is surrounded by banana and pineapple plantations. Many people go there to visit as a starting point to get to the Bay Islands. La Ceiba got its name from a large ceiba or silk-cotton tree that used to stand on the coast. Traders used to congregate there to buy and sell in the shade of the big tree.

COLONIAL TOWNS Many towns in Honduras were established in the Spanish colonial period. A few grew to the extent that they are now important for government, industrial, or commercial reasons. Other towns are better known as colonial heritage sites.

Comayagua, about 40 miles (65 km) northwest of Tegucigalpa, was the second capital of Honduras. It is famous for having numerous churches, including the Iglesia la Merced, the first church built in the country.

Considered the center for western Honduras, Santa Rosa de Copán is surrounded by mountains and national parks. It is a small, cool, very Spanish mountain town with a 200-year-old church, cobblestoned streets, and tile-roofed houses. It was once famous for its tobacco farms, but today it is better known for its coffee.

Suyapa, just outside the capital, is called the religious capital of Honduras. A legend here tells of the miraculous discovery by a peasant of a tiny clay statue of the Virgin of Suyapa, the patron saint of Honduras.

Trujillo, sited close to where Christopher Columbus first landed on mainland America, was the first capital of Honduras. Spaniards fought off pirates from a Spanish fort there. The ruins of this fort overlook the bay.

HISTORY

MUCH OF HONDURAN HISTORY is characterized by an uphill battle to bring together diverse peoples and cultures with assorted languages to create a unified nation. The mountainous geography made it difficult for groups who settled in different areas to communicate, and therefore it took a long time for cultures to form similarities that would eventually evolve into a Honduran culture. On top of this adversity, Honduras has been poor, by modern standards, for most of its existence. Despite these obstacles, there is more evidence of peace than trouble in the history of the country, compared to its Central American neighbors.

PRE-COLUMBIAN SOCIETY

Because Central America is a midway point between North and South America, people of various cultures have passed through over the centuries. Many of them eventually settled down in this region. Before Europeans reached Honduras, the land was populated by groups of people who spoke unrelated languages and whose customs were disparate.

Over 10,000 years ago, people first arrived from, possibly, Asia or Polynesia. These first settlers were probably hunters who lived in caves and simple dwellings. Thousands of years later agriculture was introduced. The first crop was probably corn, still a staple today.

Of the early inhabitants, the most advanced and notable were related to the Maya of the Yucatán and Guatemala. The Mayan civilization reached Honduras in the fifth century A.D. and spread rapidly through the Río

Above: **Petroglyphs near a cave dwelling in the region of La Paz.**

Opposite: **Intricately carved stelae in Copán's Great Plaza; the one in the foreground is believed to be an image of a queen. The Copán stelae are monuments to royalty.**

Above: **A sculptured head found at the Copán ruins.**

Right: **The Mayan ball court at the Copán ruins is the second-largest in Central America. One of the most remarkable features of the ball court is a hieroglyphic stairway illustrating the history of the Copán royal house.**

Motagua Valley in western Honduras. The Maya established extensive networks of trade throughout the region, spanning as far as central Mexico. The money of the Maya was probably the cacao bean, still a local product. The ancient western Honduran city of Copán became a center for Mayan astronomical studies, mathematics, and art. One of the longest hieroglyphic inscriptions was found at Copán.

Copán was apparently abandoned at the height of Mayan civilization. Many Maya stayed in the region, but the high priests and rulers suddenly vanished. From this point, Honduras became dominated by one indigenous group after another. These groups were often hostile toward one another. Because the different indigenous groups were always fighting for power, there was no distinct major city or authority at the time of conquest by the Spanish. By subduing and allying themselves with different groups, the Spanish were able to conquer Honduras.

SPANISH CONQUEST

Initial contact with the Spanish occurred during the final voyage in 1502 of Christopher Columbus' Spanish expedition. He sailed past the Bay Islands, and it is believed he had contact with indigenous nobility there. He then sailed on to the mainland coast of Central America and set foot in Punta Caxinas on August 14, 1502. He named the place "Honduras," a loose translation of "deep waters," a reference to the depth of the bay off the north coast. There was little European exploration of Honduras for the next two decades.

Interest in Honduras only began as a result of rivalries among Spanish military leaders in Central America, who were too far away from the emperor in Spain for the latter to govern. An expedition headed south from Panama, and in 1523, Gil González Dávila discovered and named the Gulf of Fonseca in honor of the Spanish Bishop Juan Rodríguez de Fonseca. Expeditions organized by Hernán Cortés also came from Mexico. One of these expeditions, headed by Cristóbal de Olid, first conquered Honduran territory and established a settlement there on May 3, 1524.

Rival Spanish expeditions invaded Honduras and battled to establish supremacy, not only with the indigenous people, but among themselves. Cortés himself left Mexico in 1524 to attend to the conflict in Honduras and establish his authority. He temporarily restored some order by gaining the submission of a few indigenous chiefs and began creating Spanish towns. However, the strife resumed as soon as he left nearly two years later.

Hernán Cortés (1485–1547) was one of the first Spaniards to attempt governing Honduras.

COLONIAL PERIOD

By the early 1530s, the indigenous people were being decimated by disease, mistreatment, and deportation to the Caribbean Islands as slaves.

The discovery of gold and silver in Honduras in 1536 attracted new settlers who demanded indigenous labor for their mines. This enforced labor led to a major uprising by the indigenous people led by Lempira, a young chieftain of the Lenca tribe. His courage inspired many other indigenous groups to revolt and the battle raged for two years. Lempira was eventually murdered. He is a national hero. The monetary unit of Honduras was later named after him.

Indigenous resistance died down with the defeat of Lempira's revolt, which had also contributed to the increased decimation of the native population. In 1539 an estimated 15,000 indigenous people were under Spanish control, but two years later there were only approximately 8,000 remaining.

Comayagua was made the capital in 1537, replacing Trujillo. Settlement of Honduras expanded in the 1540s as the fighting among rival Spaniards decreased, and the first bishop of Honduras was named. The key economic activity was mining for gold and silver, but some cattle ranching began as well. The indigenous

Above: **The fort of San Cristóbal at Gracias.**

Opposite: **Gracias, a town settled in 1536 by the brother of Spanish conquistador Pedro de Alvarado.**

people who were brought to work in the mines came from different villages all over the region. Because the indigenous population was so small and the Spanish wanted a larger labor force, African slaves were introduced. Everyone was forced to communicate in the language of the masters—Spanish. The old ways were mixed with the new Spanish ways and a new culture was born.

Mining began to decline in the 1560s. Honduras became a province of the Captaincy General of Guatemala and remained so until independence from Spain in 1821. A silver strike in the 1570s briefly revived the economy, and Tegucigalpa began to rival Comayagua in size and importance. Mining efforts were hampered by the limited size of gold and silver deposits, a lack of capital and labor, the rugged terrain, and bureaucratic regulations and incompetence. By the 17th century, Honduras had become neglected and poor. A major problem for the Spanish was the English pirates along the Caribbean coast during the 17th century. Eventually, the English began to settle on the Bay Islands and along the coast. Spain regained control of the Caribbean coast, but the English settlers remained.

Miguel Angel Matutte's painting shows a martial General Francisco Morazán (left) and a scholarly José Cecilio del Valle.

INDEPENDENCE

The early years of independence were characterized by political instability. The long-standing rivalry between Tegucigalpa and Comayagua kept the people of Honduras divided. Following independence from Spain in 1821, Honduras and the other Central American countries were still joined to the Mexican empire. In 1823 they broke away from Mexican rule and established the United Provinces of Central America with its capital in Guatemala City. The first president elected was Manuel José Arce, in 1825. Francisco Morazán, a Honduran military hero, was elected president of the federation in 1830. In 1834 he moved the capital of the federation to San Salvador.

The 1830s saw constant conflict between the Liberal and Conservative parties of the region. After a revolt by the Conservatives led by Rafael Carrera in 1838, the federation was dissolved. Honduras declared independence on November 15, 1838. By January 1839 it had adopted a constitution, although there was little sense of nationhood. All attempts to restore the federation after this 1838 split failed.

For Honduras, the period of federation had been a time of local rivalries, ideological disputes, political chaos, and disruption of its already fragile economy. Its instability attracted ambitious politicians from within and outside Central America. For most of the rest of the 19th century El Salvador, Guatemala, and Nicaragua interfered in Honduras' internal affairs. Six constitutions were implemented and presidents were imposed and deposed by Nicaragua and Guatemala. The frequent changes of government increased Honduras' instability. British influence increased and then decreased when American interest in Honduras flourished.

FRANCISCO MORAZÁN

Francisco Morazán (1792–1842) served as president of the United Provinces of Central America for two terms and is considered the father of Central America for his major role in defending the original union of the five states that now make up Central America. Streets, parks, and cities are named after him throughout the region.

Morazán was born in Tegucigalpa. He received little formal schooling but educated himself sufficiently to practice law and secure a position in the municipal government of Tegucigalpa, where his political career began.

In 1827 he led his Liberal Party against the army of the Conservative Party, defeating it in 1829. The following year he was elected president of the United Provinces of Central America. He started radical programs to improve education and the justice system, and attempted to promote economic development for the region. His plans for reform included reducing the influence of the Roman Catholic Church in state affairs.

Morazán struggled to strengthen the federation, but the disputes increased, and his dream of a united, harmonious alliance ended in 1838. He was executed in 1842 after an attempt to restore the federation.

JOSÉ TRINIDAD CABAÑAS

Cabañas (1805–71) is considered a hero for his attempts to reunite the Central American federal government. He was president of Honduras for two separate terms—March 1 to July 6, 1852, and December 31, 1853 to June 6, 1855. Cabañas was born a creole, the son of José María Cabañas and Juana María Faillos. Cabañas was a Liberal politician whose role in Honduran history began during the civil war of 1826–29 when he was second-in-command to Francisco Morazán.

His second term as president was noteworthy for the very first attempt at building a railroad in Central America. He was supported by the common Honduran people, but his liberal beliefs and their support were not acceptable to the Conservatives then holding power in Guatemala. Interference in Guatemalan affairs led to his overthrow by the Guatemalans in 1855.

Cabañas fled to El Salvador where he remained politically active. He was responsible for a political uprising in El Salvador as late as 1865.

José Cecilio del Valle is considered a hero in Honduras. He wrote the declaration of Central America's independence from Spain in 1821.

Chiquita Brands containers at La Lima, loaded with bananas, await departure for the port of Puerto Cortés.

BANANAS

At the end of the 1800s, banana traders in New Orleans looked to Honduras as a reliable supplier of commercially grown bananas and founded the Standard Fruit Company. In the north, along the Caribbean coast, banana plantations began operation. Honduras soon became the world's leading exporter of bananas. The banana companies became more important than the government for many Hondurans because of their domination of commercial life in the area and worker welfare system. Bananas remained the mainstay of the modern economy for many years.

In Tegucigalpa, power remained unstable and revolts repeatedly broke out against the government. Nicaragua became increasingly involved in Honduras in the early 20th century. When its army invaded the country in 1911, the US government intervened to protect the North American banana trade—President William Howard Taft sent US Marines to Puerto Cortés.

In 1923 the election for a new president produced no majority for any candidate, leaving the country on the brink of civil war. The United States stepped in again, and a new election was held in which the National Party took power. In 1932 General Tiburcio Carías Andino became president in a peaceful, fair election and remained in power until 1948, ruling with an authoritarian hand. Early in the Carías regime, Panama disease dramatically damaged the banana industry, while the Depression and World War II cut off the banana trade and the fruit rotted on the docks.

In 1954 banana workers became dissatisfied and went on strike, causing a severe strain on the nation's economy. Initial government efforts to end the strike failed and work stoppages spread to other industries. The strike ended when workers were granted significantly increased benefits and gained recognition of their right to bargain. The strike decreased the power of the fruit companies.

When the banana industry in Honduras faced difficulties caused by disease and war, the government diversified the economy into mining, cattle ranching, timber exports, and coffee production to make it less vulnerable.

THE GREAT BANANA STRIKE

In 1954 Honduran workers at a Caribbean port asked for overtime wages for loading bananas onto a boat on a Sunday. Their request was refused, but they loaded the boat anyway. The following Sunday, a similar incident occurred. Officials noticed a slowdown in work but foolishly ignored it. As the unrest grew, President Juan Manuel Gálvez became concerned and sent soldiers to the Caribbean coast. This action angered the workers, and within a week one banana company had lost all its workers. The strike spread to other banana companies, a tobacco plant, a mining company, and several clothing factories, all American-owned. The strikers held out for three months. When officials finally made concessions, work resumed with shorter hours, overtime pay, medical benefits, and paid vacations. Workers in Honduras had learned that they were a powerful political force.

MODERN HONDURAS

After the military coup in 1963, Honduras was ruled by military governments for two decades. The five Honduran governments since the 1981 general election have all been democratically elected. Four of them were Liberal Party governments.

In 1957, yet another constitution was enacted and Ramón Villeda Morales of the Liberal Party became president. Under Villeda, many schools were built and labor rights were strengthened. A social security system was installed but it provided the medical needs and pensions of only a limited number of workers. During this time, the Central American Common Market was formed and trade restrictions on imports were lifted. Many products that used to be imported were now regionally made. However, because Honduras lacked roads, a railway system, and sophisticated investors, most of these factories were established in Guatemala, El Salvador, and Costa Rica—Honduras was left behind.

On October 3, 1963, a military coup put Air Force Colonel Osvaldo López Arellano in power. Congress was dissolved, the constitution was suspended, and planned elections were canceled. The United States promptly broke diplomatic relations with Honduras. In 1978 a new junta headed by General Policarpo Paz García seized the government with a promise to return Honduras to civilian rule. In April 1980 military rule began to wind down; a constituent assembly was convened and an election was planned.

Meanwhile violent revolutions were occurring in Nicaragua and El Salvador. Because Honduras is located between El Salvador and Nicaragua and has a history of poverty and democratic instability, it drew involvement from the United States. Weapons poured into Honduras in response to the Sandinista victory in Nicaragua, and Americans staged military maneuvers in Honduras. After the conflict, the decrease in American military spending in Honduras left the country in an economic crisis once again. Rafael Leonardo Callejas of the National Party scored a clear victory in the 1989 election, and he began to deal with the economic situation.

The rising cost of living caused his party to be defeated in the 1993 election. Carlos Roberto Reina of the Liberal Party, who became president, continued the work begun by Callejas. He was succeeded in January 1998 by Carlos Roberto Flores Facusse, also of the Liberal Party.

Just when the political climate appeared to have settled, calamity struck in the shape of Hurricane Mitch in November 1998. The devastation caused by the hurricane left Honduras in dire straits. Damage to fertile lands lowered the outlook for agricultural exports, and the country will be rebuilding its infrastructure for the next few years. At the same time, this is an opportunity to rebuild a more efficient country.

THE SOCCER WAR

Border disputes have long been a problem in Central America. Honduras has rarely been the aggressor, but in 1969 a border dispute with El Salvador erupted into a brief war. The Honduran government believed that Salvadorans had taken advantage of the open border with Honduras and had gained property under the agrarian reforms taking place in Honduras. This land was only supposed to go to people who were Honduran by birth.

The dispute is termed the Soccer War because at the time, Honduras and El Salvador were engaged in a three-game elimination match for the World Cup preliminaries. Violent encounters erupted at the games, and both countries were insulted and enraged. Honduras decided to suspend trade with El Salvador. The territorial dispute was finally resolved by the World Court in 1992. The picture here is of detained Salvadorans with a Honduran guard after the Soccer War.

GOVERNMENT

HONDURAS HAS HAD A HISTORY of nearly constant unstable government. From the early indigenous groups continually fighting for dominance, to the Spanish explorers battling each other and the British for power, to the military twice seizing the presidency, politics in Honduras has matured.

Since January 1982, when the military turned the nation over to a democratically elected president and congress, national elections have come to be celebrated in a festive manner. Hondurans are optimistic about a more stable future.

NATIONAL GOVERNMENT

Honduras' national government is divided into three branches: executive, legislative, and judicial. Each branch is supposed to be autonomous, but in reality the executive branch dominates the legislative and judicial branches. There is also an elections tribunal that functions as an independent division with jurisdiction throughout the country.

CONSTITUTION The present constitution of Honduras, the 16th since independence from Spain, was adopted on January 20, 1982, one week after almost 20 years of military rule ended. The Honduran constitution is seen more as a political ideal than a legal instrument.

This constitution establishes three separate branches of government and provides for an independent elections tribunal responsible for national elections. It also protects basic human rights, women's right to vote, child and labor rights, freedom of speech, freedom of the press, and issues of nationality, social security, health, education, and housing.

Above: **The Palacio Legislativo or congress building in Tegucigalpa. The Honduran constitution sets forth 45 powers of the National Congress; the most important concern the power to make, enact, interpret, and repeal laws.**

Opposite: **The Casa Presidencial, or Presidential Palace, shows a strong Spanish-colonial influence.**

The Honduran coat of arms consists of a Mayan pyramid with towers and a volcano centered under a sun and a rainbow. It is backed by cornucopias showing native products and a quiver of arrows symbolizing Indian arms. The seal is supported by a mining and forest landscape (pines and oak trees) with a miner's and a woodsman's tools. Around the oval central seal are the words *República de Honduras: Libre, soberana e independente* ("Republic of Honduras: Free, sovereign, and independent) and the date of independence, September 15, 1821.

THE EXECUTIVE BRANCH is headed by the president who is assisted by at least 12 cabinet ministers. The president is elected by a simple majority every four years and may not run for a succeeding term. The responsibilities of the president include organizing, directing, and promoting economic, education, health, and foreign policies. The president has the power to veto or sanction laws approved by the National Congress with a few exceptions, such as constitutional amendments. The president is also given the military title of General Commander.

THE LEGISLATIVE BRANCH consists of the unicameral National Congress—128 deputies elected every four years at the same time as the president. The National Congress conducts legislative functions during regular annual sessions from January to October. Its roles are to approve choices of the president, appoint committees to study issues that come before the legislature, elect the numerous government officials, and approve the national budget, international treaties, and taxes.

THE JUDICIAL BRANCH of the government consists of the Supreme Court of Justice, courts of appeal, courts of first instance, and justices of the peace. The Supreme Court is a court of last resort. It has 14 constitutional powers and duties and is divided into three chambers—civil, criminal, and labor—with three justices assigned to each chamber. Courts of appeal have three-judge panels who hear appeals from all lower courts. The courts of first instance serve as trial courts for serious civil and criminal cases. Justices of the peace serve in each department of the country as investigators of minor cases.

THE NATIONAL ELECTIONS TRIBUNAL Since Honduras returned to civilian democratic rule in 1982, national elections have been held every four years to elect the president, the National Congress, and municipal

Freedom of speech is guaranteed by the Honduran constitution and includes the right to demonstrate.

officials. This tribunal is an autonomous and independent body responsible for organizing and conducting elections. The National Registry of Persons works under the National Elections Tribunal and is responsible for issuing identity cards to all Hondurans (these are also voter registration cards) and conducting a census before each election.

LOCAL GOVERNMENT

Honduras is divided into 18 departments (provinces), which are subdivided into 291 municipalities. A municipality may include more than one city. There is also a Central District consisting of Tegucigalpa and Comayagüela. The president freely appoints and removes governors for each department. Departmental governors are an extension of the executive branch of the national government. Each governor may freely appoint or remove a secretary to assist him or her. A municipality is administered by a mayor and council elected every four years at the same time as the president. The council varies in size depending on the population of the municipality.

POLITICAL PARTIES

Two parties have been traditionally dominant—the Liberal Party of Honduras (PLH) and the National Party of Honduras (PNH). These were the only two official parties from 1902 to 1948; this factor laid the groundwork for the present-day two-party system. The PLH was established in 1891 under the leadership of Policarpo Bonilla Vásquez and had its origins in the liberal reform efforts of the late 19th century. The PNH was formed in 1902 when a group broke off from the PLH. In 1963 it became aligned with the military.

Since the 1980s, two small parties have emerged—Pinu and the Christian Democratic Party of Honduras (PDCH). They have participated in the national and legislative elections, but neither party has posed a threat to the political domination of the PLH and the PNH.

ROLE OF THE MILITARY

Since the return to civilian democratic rule in 1982, the military's influence has been slowly receding. The military was a powerful force in domestic politics beginning in the 1950s. It usurped the presidency in 1963 and held it until 1971. In 1972 the military took power again and kept it another 10 years. Today, the internal workings of the two dominant parties appear free from military influence. However, the military has had an increasing influence in the nation's economic activities.

POLITICS TODAY

Today, Honduran politics is heavily influenced by a variety of special interest groups and political organizations that often help to resolve conflicts. Such groups include business organizations such as the banana

There are few ideological differences between the Liberal Party and the National Party in Honduras, and allegiance to one group or the other is still often based on family traditions. The Liberal Party is stronger in urban areas and the more developed northern departments. The National Party, on the other hand, is stronger in more rural areas and the less developed southern agricultural departments.

companies, labor and peasant groups, and popular, legally recognized groups—student, women's, human rights, and environmental groups. The government has started to hold the military accountable for human rights violations and has begun rooting out corruption in government organizations.

WOMEN IN POLITICS

The first women's group in Honduras was the Women's Cultural Society, formed in 1923. This group fought for economic and political rights for women. But it was not until 1954 that the fight for the right to vote succeeded. Honduras was the last Latin American country to give women suffrage. Women were also active in the formation of the labor movement and took part in the great banana strike of 1954. By the late 1980s women were represented at all levels of government, although their numbers were few. Women have held seats in the National Congress and the Supreme Court, high-level executive-branch positions, mayorships, and both the National Party and the Liberal Party have supported women's nominations for presidential candidates.

Visitación Padilla (1882–1960)

Padilla was a strong, ambitious, articulate woman in Honduras during the early 1900s. She started out as a schoolteacher and soon became Honduras' first female journalist. As a feminist, she was certainly a pioneer in Central America and became the best-known feminist figure in Honduras. She felt the necessity to draw women together to fight for what they believed in and for what they needed. Padilla became president of the Women's Cultural Society, which led the struggle for women's economic and political rights. She also became involved in heated governmental politics where she worked for peace during the troubled years of the early 20th century. In 1924, the United States was planning to send the Marines into Honduras to help settle the political problems in Central America. Padilla cofounded the Boletin de Defensa Nacional, which led the protest against US intervention.

A recently formed women's group has named itself the Visitación Padilla Committee in honor of this redoubtable woman. The committee is dedicated to building a peaceful future for the children of Honduras.

ECONOMY

HONDURAS IS ONE of the poorest, underdeveloped countries in the Western Hemisphere. Hondurans work under difficult conditions for very little income. The economy is divided geographically between the highlands and the lowlands. The people of the highlands contribute to the nation's economy mainly with subsistence farming, raising livestock, and mining. In the lowlands, the chief occupations are in the plantations.

The political turbulence that has plagued Honduras and its Central American neighbors has negatively affected the Honduran economy, which is in need of capital and technical know-how. The economy was also greatly affected by the damage of Hurricane Mitch in November 1998 to important export crops. More than 60% of the year's fruit crop was obliterated. Hondurans have begun the long, hard work to bring their country back to its previous level of industry and hope to develop well beyond that as they rebuild and replan their nation's economy.

Opposite: **A worker puts a coat of varnish on a door made of different kinds of timber. The government manages the timber industry to prevent wasteful practices.**

Left: **Drying tobacco on racks on wheels.**

41

Women sorting coffee beans drying in the sun.

EXPORTS

The economy of Honduras still relies primarily on one export: bananas. As with any underdeveloped country that depends on one export, the Honduran economy is at the mercy of world prices. However, the government is increasing its involvement in the economy and diversifying exports in order to develop a more stable economy. Today, coffee is the second most profitable export. Beef had the potential to become a very important export in the 1980s, but because of high production costs, the livestock industry now accounts for less than 3% of total exports, yet it is still an important export. Honduras also exports cotton, tobacco, pineapples, sugarcane, vegetables, and shrimp.

PRIMARY OCCUPATIONS AND INDUSTRIES

The Honduran labor force is composed of mainly unskilled and uneducated laborers. More than half the rural population is landless and relies on seasonal labor with low wages.

Men sawing logs in a sawmill in Teguolgalpa.

AGRICULTURE Because of the rugged, mountainous country, only 15% of the land in Honduras is arable, yet agriculture contributes the most to the gross domestic product (GDP) and employs 60% of the labor force. In the highlands and Pacific lowlands, ranching provides employment and livestock products for export. Large agribusinesses take up much of the arable highlands. The remainder is divided between subsistence farmers, 55% of whom have less than five acres (two hectares) of mediocre farmland and earn less than US$70 per year from those small plots.

In the Caribbean coastal area, a different type of agriculture is practiced. Two large US companies, United Brands and Standard Fruit and Steamship Company, hold over half of the arable land. These companies produce a substantial part of the national income growing bananas for export.

FORESTRY Honduras was once famous for its mahogany trees, but now pine is the main commercial forest product. Because Honduras has extensive pine forests, forestry has the potential to contribute a large source of income. However, the industry has been badly abused. Large tracts have been cleared for agriculture, especially cattle ranches, and commercial timber exploitation has been inefficient. Many trees felled for lumber do not reach sawmills, and not all that do are processed. In 1974 the government put all forests into state ownership for more efficient forestry management, but forests are still disappearing rapidly through wasteful practices.

FISHING is still a small industry, but it is developing along the Caribbean coast. The largest catch is of shrimp, most of which is exported to the United States.

MINING produced the main exports in the late 1800s, but declined rapidly in importance during the 1900s. The largest mining company, the New York and Honduras Rosario Mining Company, produced US$60 million worth of gold and silver from 1882 to 1954 before discontinuing most of its operations. Mining's contribution to the GDP declined steadily during the 1980s to account for only 2% of the GDP in 1992. Yet Honduras remains the country richest in mineral resources in Central America. Gold, silver, lead, zinc, and cadmium are mined and exported to the United States and Europe.

MANUFACTURING employed only 9–13% of workers in 1993. Small Honduran shops make mostly clothing and food products. Asian-owned textile industries have begun to dominate the smaller domestic manufacturing economy, creating jobs at a relatively high wage of $4 per day and thereby alleviating a little the unemployment problem.

SERVICES About one-third of the population of Honduras works in the service industry. Most of them are employed as domestic help in the cities.

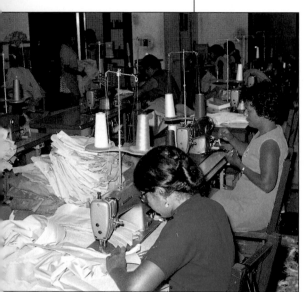

Women at their sewing machines in a clothing factory.

TOURISM is just beginning to develop in Honduras. There are many beautiful natural attractions, most of them pristine and unspoiled. Foreigners are attracted to Honduras by the Mayan ruins in Copán and the outstanding coral reef off the Bay Islands. Small ecotourism projects are considered to have significant potential, especially in the Bay Islands.

ENERGY SOURCES

For many years, Hondurans have relied on fuelwood and biomass, mostly waste products from agricultural production, to supply them with energy. These sources have generally met approximately 70% of the country's total energy demand. Petroleum has never been produced in Honduras, so the

The General Francisco Morazán Dam at El Cajón Reservoir.

country has relied on oil imports to fill much of its energy needs. About 13% of total export earnings are spent on purchasing oil. Honduran use of electricity is low, as less than 50% of those in rural areas have access to utilities, but electricity production is increasing slowly with demand.

TELECOMMUNICATIONS

The telecommunications system in Honduras is largely outdated and poorly maintained. As of 1993, the entire country had only 35,100 telephones, fewer than seven per 1,000 inhabitants. Service is limited to government offices, businesses, and homes of the upper class. Half the phones are in Tegucigalpa, a quarter in San Pedro Sula, and the remainder are scattered all over the country in large towns. Telephones, as well as telegraph machines, telex, and fax services are offered at offices of the

A postal worker chats with a resident in Valle de Angeles, just 16 miles (25 km) outside Tegucigalpa.

Maximizing auto facilities on the road through La Esperanza in western Honduras.

Honduran phone company, Hondutel, in towns. There are phone booths painted bright red outside these offices and on busy street corners for local phone calls. Some smaller towns do not have a single telephone. There is, however, a low-capacity radio-relay system and a rather unreliable open-wire network with switchboards in towns that have no phones.

Television sets are still rare. There are 11 television stations in the larger cities and 17 low-power transmitters in small towns. Radio is the primary mode of getting information to Hondurans. All parts of the country are in the range of at least one radio station. Many families sit around the radio in the evenings to listen to the news or stories.

TRANSPORTATION

Because of the mountainous terrain, there has been difficulty creating a transportation system to meet the entire country's needs. In 1993 Honduras had just over 4,000 miles (6,500 km) of roads, only 770 miles (1,240 km) of which were paved. Most of these roads connect the ports and industrial areas. Only one paved highway joins the Caribbean and the Pacific, passing through Puerto Cortés, San Pedro Sula, and Tegucigalpa. This major, significant highway was covered and badly damaged by Hurricane Mitch in November 1998, but it was the first road to be rebuilt. Other areas, served only by gravel and dirt roads often impassable during even moderately rainy weather, were accessible only by air after the storm. The government plans to pave many of these roads as they are reconstructed across Honduras.

The railroads were built by the original banana companies for transporting bananas to ports, not for transporting goods and passengers nationwide. Two rail systems provide freight and passenger service, and both are located in the north-central and northwestern coastal areas. Tegucigalpa remains the only Spanish-speaking capital in the Americas with no rail service whatsoever.

Above: **Old tires make convenient spare parts for this horse-drawn cart in San Pedro Sula.**

Right: **All aboard for Puerto Cortés from Tela. The north coast train service links these two cities with San Pedro Sula.**

Three ports handle Honduras' seaborne trade. Most of the agricultural exports and imports of petroleum and manufactured products pass through Puerto Cortés.

Lack of alternative transportation through Honduras' mountains makes air travel important. There are two international airports—in Tegucigalpa and near San Pedro Sula. Domestic flights operate between the two cities and to Roatán. There is also air service to rural areas where planes land on small, unpaved fields.

CURRENCY

The unit of currency is the lempira, and there are 100 centavos in a lempira. Paper bills of one, two, five, 10, 20, 50, and 100 lempiras and coins for one, two, five, 10, and 20 centavos are available.

WAGES

Each industry has its own minimum wage based on an eight-hour day shift. Production, processing, or trade of products such as tobacco, bananas, coffee, and seafood offer the highest minimum wage of 39.65 lempiras (US$3) a day. Workers in insurance and financial services make 36 lempiras (US$2.70) a day. Agriculture, forestry, and fishing workers have the lowest minimum wage—30 lempiras (US$2.25) a day.

Overtime is paid for a shift of over eight hours, and the rate is higher if overtime hours occur during the night or are an extension of the night shift. In June each year, workers receive a month's wages as a bonus for a full year's work.

Lempira notes carry the Honduran coat of arms. Francisco Morazán is on the five lempira bill and José Trinidad Cabañas is on the 10 lempira bill.

HONDURANS

THE POPULATION OF HONDURAS is 5.8 million. Approximately 44% live in the cities, while the rest live in rural areas centered around small villages or towns. About 90% of the population is *mestizo* ("mes-TEE-zoh"), people who are a racial mix of indigenous and European ancestry. The remaining inhabitants include indigenous peoples (4%), blacks from Africa and the Caribbean Islands (5%), whites, mostly from Europe (1%), and a small number of immigrants from the Middle East.

Above: **Ladinos returning from work.**

Opposite: **A Garifuna (or Black Carib) child whose ancestors probably came from the Caribbean Islands.**

ETHNIC GROUPS

Mestizos, whites, and most blacks are Ladino ("lah-DEE-noh")—people who speak Spanish and whose lifestyle follows Hispanic cultural patterns. Most Ladinos are members of the Roman Catholic Church. Their socioeconomic status ranges from poor subsistence farmers to business people in the cities. In general, family counts for everything. These close family connections make it difficult for immigrants to penetrate Ladino culture, so different and separate subcultures of immigrants exist in the cities of Honduras. This lack of ethnic mixing may seem surprising because almost all Ladinos themselves have a mixed racial ancestry. It is not that they are unfriendly. Ladinos simply value their extended families above all else, and so remain tightknit groups.

INDIGENOUS HONDURANS

Since colonial times, there has been intermarriage between native Hondurans and Spanish people. The remaining indigenous population consists of many different small groups who maintain customs set apart from Ladino culture.

Lenca women in La Paz.

LENCA One of the largest remaining indigenous groups in Honduras is the Lenca, who are believed to have descended from the ancient Maya. They live in the southwestern interior. Lenca women buy and sell vegetables in a market at La Esperanza-Intibucá and in Marcala.

The Lenca still practice some traditional customs. They cultivate communal lands instead of owning private plots and use digging sticks instead of plows. Women wear a long skirt and short blouse similar to those worn by women in colonial days. They usually work alongside the men in the fields. Other characteristics that set the Lenca apart are their festival dances, basket-weaving, pottery, and home brewing of the traditional liquor, *chicha*.

They have adopted some aspects of the Ladino national culture. The Lenca are Catholic, although they are more religious than the average Ladino, and they no longer speak their native language but dialects that have borrowed Spanish words. For these reasons, there has been some debate as to whether the Lenca can be considered truly indigenous.

CHORTÍ INDIANS, another group with a Mayan heritage, live mostly near the town of Copán. Chortí villagers grow crops and trade in handicraft. They are skilled makers of woven baskets, pottery, soap, wooden products, and leather goods.

JICAQUE In the past, northern indigenous groups were less settled than those living in the mountainous southwest. These groups were basically hunters and fishers. One northern group, the Jicaque, once inhabited the Caribbean coast until they were driven inland where they began to settle and cultivate corn like the western Indians. Only a few hundred maintain their language and traditions. They dress in old-style tunics. Their homes are distinctive, made of planks tied with vines and roofed with thatch. They still hunt with blowguns.

This Lenca home is built in a clearing separated from the wilderness by a roughly constructed fence.

MISKITO The Miskito Indians are an isolated group who live harmoniously in the Mosquito Coast in northeastern Honduras. The area was essentially ignored by the Spanish, so the Miskito were left to themselves, more so than the rest of Honduras. They are related to Indians in South America with whom they share a similar language.

There has been intermarriage between the Miskito and blacks, often escaped slaves who sought the north coast for refuge. The Miskito today are a racially mixed population of indigenous, African, and European origin, mostly British. Many still speak a creole language with contributions from Spanish, English, and German. They are generally considered by Hondurans to be indigenous.

Miskito cultivate yucca, beans, and corn in shifting agriculture. They burn and clear plots, then move on when the land is exhausted, leaving it to replenish itself. They also raise livestock such as chickens, pigs, and cows.

Because the Miskito live on the coast and rely on waterways for transportation, they have developed dugout and flatbottom boats. Fishing is important to their livelihood. Some Miskito stun their catch with arrows poisoned with an extract from jungle vines.

CHOROTEGA, PIPIL, PAYA, AND PECH These few other indigenous groups number only a couple of hundred people. The Chorotega migrated from Mexico in pre-Columbian times and have retained many of their religious and cultural traits. The Pipil, who are of Nahuatl descent, live along the southwestern mountain slopes.

The exact origin of the Paya is unknown but their ancestors are believed to have come from South America. They live in the lush and humid river regions of the Mosquito Coast, many near the Río Plátano, working as subsistence farmers and fishermen. They use farming tools, fishing poles, and spears that they make themselves.

The Pech, another indigenous group of the Mosquito Coast, are believed to be descendants of the Paya. The Pech men fish, and women tend to crops and livestock. Pech children now go to Pech schools during the day but still help their parents before and after school.

Both the Paya and the Pech are proud people with fascinating customs, skills, and knowledge. From the forest and river they get food, shelter, and medicine, and fulfill every other need. In return, they conserve and protect the forest and river as their ancestors have for hundreds of years.

Left: **A Pech man and his daughter.**

Opposite: **Miskito Indian women and children in the Biosfera del Río Plátano.**

Above and opposite: **Black Carib or Garifuna.**

BLACKS

Two distinct groups of blacks have settled in Honduras: the Black Carib, known as the Garifuna, and the black population in the Bay Islands.

The Black Carib settled in coastal villages along the Caribbean coast in the early 1800s. They are descendants of freed African slaves who were deported by the British in 1797 from the island of St. Vincent in the Caribbean. They speak a Carib-based creole.

The Black Carib share many customs with the Miskito Indians. Both groups have been self-sufficient through farming and fishing for generations, but today, many of the men have to work outside the region to supplement an income that has been reduced by a loss of land. Many families are split up for long periods of time.

The black population on the Bay Islands is black and black and white mixed. These people have descended from English-speaking blacks and whites from Belize and the Cayman Islands. Their traditions are distinctly West Indian and they speak creole or Caribbean English.

ARABS

There is a thriving Arab community in Honduras descended from immigrants who arrived in the early 1900s, mostly from Palestine and Lebanon. The Arabs have remained culturally distinct by keeping many of their own traditions alive. They were first successful as merchants and then moved to the industrial cities where they have become economically quite powerful.

SOCIAL HIERARCHY

Like other Central American countries, Honduras has an uneven distribution of wealth. The minority of the population controls the wealth and politics. The majority is made up of poverty-stricken subsistence farmers, hired hands on large corporate farms, and low-paid laborers in the cities. Since the 1950s, however, a small middle class has also emerged. There is little social conflict between the classes, but the increasing poverty of the majority and an increase in the wealth and power of the upper class is a concern today.

UPPER CLASS The Honduran elite is divided into two basic groups—the traditional elite, who were originally owners of large rural estates, and the military elite. The traditional elite were *hacendados* ("hah-sen-DAH-dohs"), the owners of large haciendas in the interior highlands and valleys. Many still live on their estates. After World War II, this group of wealthy landowners became involved in cattle production in response to the increase in the beef market. However, the land they used for cattle ranching—ultimately to export food to other countries—had originally been used for domestic food production. Therefore, social tensions increased in rural Honduras between the upper and lower classes.

This group of wealthy people is not particularly cohesive. There are split interests over political and economic issues. Many of them have competing businesses. Politically, there are as many Conservatives as there are Liberals. Some Liberals support and work toward the social change that middle and lower classes have sought over the years.

The military elite emerged in the mid-1950s when the armed forces underwent a major transformation. The military went from being a variety of provincial militia groups to a US-trained national institution. Because the traditional elite did not favor this military institution, the two groups have remained distinct. Possibly as a result of this separation of interest between the two elite groups, neither has become overwhelmingly powerful.

Children from upper- and middle-class Honduran families dress much like children in urban Western societies.

MIDDLE CLASS The small group that makes up the middle class is growing at a steady pace and is mostly settled in the cities. People who are considered middle-class are those with a higher education—college students, professors, teachers, civil servants, engineers, and merchants. On the Caribbean coast, the growth of the middle class was directly related to the area's industrial and business enterprises. In the north, the success of merchants was due to the market demands created by employed workers in the area's agribusiness. Although the middle class makes a decent income compared to the lower class, their income is still low compared to North American standards.

This group is still small because growth in industry and commerce is slow. Job opportunities are scarce, but many people move to the cities every year seeking to end their poverty and hoping to join the middle class. Many middle-class citizens are involved in the politics of social change. They create and join unions, church groups, and other political organizations.

LOWER CLASS The lower class is divided into two groups based on where they live. Traditionally, the poor of Honduras have been the peasants in rural areas, but there is a growing lower class in the cities. Peasants are subsistence farmers called *campesinos* ("kahm-pay-SEE-nos") who make a living off their land.

Children of the rural poor in the south.

Today, because so much land has been absorbed by commercial agribusiness, family subsistence off the land is difficult. This situation began after the 1950s when cattle and cotton production for export increased, and land was absorbed into large agribusinesses. When the small plots of land were no longer enough to support the family, people either went to work on nearby large farms or migrated to the cities in search of employment.

The urban poor is now made up of many of the campesinos who moved to cities looking for employment opportunities. This has created a very large population of impoverished, unemployed people looking for work and living on the streets in cities like Tegucigalpa and San Pedro Sula. Many of those who do find work end up employed in the service industry, doing domestic work such as cleaning the homes of the wealthy. Some join the construction industry, while others join the assembly lines that manufacture products such as shoes, clothing, baskets, and furniture.

Schoolchildren in uniform in Copán.

POPULATION CHANGES

In the second half of the 20th century, there has been a major increase in the population, but the population density is still relatively low with 134 inhabitants per square mile (52 per square km). There has been significant immigration from neighboring Central American countries that have had higher levels of civil conflict. The growth of the banana industry resulted in the first major shift in population. In the early 1900s, many Hondurans moved to the Caribbean coast to seek employment on the plantations. Today, most internal migration is from rural areas to urban centers, especially the two largest cities, Tegucigalpa and San Pedro Sula. In the 1950s Tegucigalpa's population increased by 75%, causing a situation of inadequate housing and the emergence of shantytowns.

Most migrants today are in their teens or early twenties and they seek an increased standard of living outside poor family farms. Honduran men tend to move from their family land to wherever there is a developing agricultural area or to cities for work in artisan shops or as laborers in factories or construction. Women, on the other hand, have a limited choice of employment. Most migrant women are those who want to escape economic hardship and early marriage and childbearing. These women end up in the cities working as domestic help for the elite or as street vendors. Since the 1990s, women have also begun to find employment in assembly factories.

DRESS

Hondurans value physical appearance and dress formally and neatly. Ladinos wear Western-style clothes. Women usually wear a colorful dress or a skirt and blouse, while men wear long-sleeved dress shirts and slacks. Jeans with a T-shirt is considered too informal, especially outdoors in Tegucigalpa or San Pedro Sula. Children always wear uniforms to school. Public schoolchildren wear white and blue. Private schools have their own colored uniforms. The cities can look very colorful when school lets out with all the children wearing various color clothing.

Indigenous groups each have their own traditional dress. They wear clothing that varies from completely traditional dress to a mixture of Western and traditional styles.

Honduras has a wide variety of traditional folk dance costumes and many are still worn on special occasions such as the celebration of a town's patron saint's day. The Honduran post office once issued a series of stamps showing traditional dress from different parts of the country.

FOLK DRESS

Most towns have folk dance groups that wear traditional dress. A common style, originally worn by the Lencas, is all in white for men and women. The white, flowing cotton material called *manta* ("MAHN-tah") was once worn mainly by the poor, but its use has spread widely. This style of dress is considered most appropriate for dancing Lenca and mestizo dances with indigenous influences. It is also the most common clothing for typical dolls in the central region. Another very popular folk dance dress is that found in the La Paz department. Women's dresses are very brightly colored and often have shiny metallic decorations or colored ribbons that flutter as the women dance.

LIFESTYLE

HONDURAS HAS TRADITIONALLY been a farming society, and in spite of recent urban growth, it is still one of the least urbanized countries of Central America. Poor rural living conditions are of special concern, as the people are malnourished and perpetually struggling to make ends meet. Yet, families provide an important support system that keeps Hondurans relatively happy. They help one another, creating a real sense of unity.

FAMILY ROLES

The family is the cornerstone of Honduran society and culture. Extended families are close-knit, often living in one home, including not only grandparents, but also aunts, uncles, and cousins. The closest relationships are usually familial ones, and any leisure time, such as celebrating festivals, is spent with relatives. Children are taught from a young age that relatives are to be trusted, and anyone outside the family is, at least, suspect. Families provide important social support, especially for women. And when men go into business, it is usually with loyal kinsmen.

A discrepancy exists, however, between this ideal of family values and the typical Honduran family. Marriages are expensive, so many couples live together but are not legally married. Many men leave their wives, girlfriends, and children, especially in the cities. Many households are run by single mothers—41% in Tegucigalpa. Society disapproves of a man who does not support his children. Despite this, some men do not assume the responsibilities of fatherhood.

Above: **Hondurans have a strong devotion to traditional customs and to their families.**

Opposite: **Students of an agricultural school. About 60% of the labor force belongs to the agricultural sector.**

Boys and men are encouraged to participate in macho activities such as hunting.

MEN The concept of *machismo* ("mah-CHEEZ-moh") is evident throughout all socioeconomic levels. Men are expected to be macho—daring, strong, unemotional, and brave. Men prove their masculinity or machismo by flirting with women, being demanding, and acting in an aggressive way. Boys are encouraged from an early age to do whatever they please. They do not help out in the house. Any suggestion of effeminate behavior is ridiculed.

The father's role varies depending on the family, but generally fathers must be respected and obeyed. They are more removed from daily family affairs but usually have the final say in important matters. Men often do not feel a responsibility for their children, expecting women to take care of them completely. Men run the farms or send money home if they are working elsewhere.

WOMEN The female ideal of *marianismo* ("mah-ree-ahn-EEZ-moh") is to be loyal, chaste, and submissive. Girls are taught from an early age to be more emotional, more vulnerable, and less intelligent than boys.

Women are supposed to take care of their husbands or boyfriends and their children. Honduran women are strong and capable. They often work in the fields alongside men, as well as work in the kitchen.

More women are getting a higher education today, but those who do are still paid less than men for the same kind of work. Grandmothers and aunts often take care of the children so that a young mother can work outside the home or go to school.

CHILDREN are valued, honored, and cherished. They are expected to work hard at home and at school, but they are pampered as well. Generally speaking, children are valued as the next generation, and parents want their children to be better educated and have more money than they did.

However, this ideal is not completely followed when it comes to the poverty-stricken family. Children of such families are often not pampered at all, and are sometimes ignored. And the men who permanently leave their families often do not send money to their wives or girlfriends in order to provide for their children. Where a woman has children from a previous relationship, they may not be cared for by her new husband or boyfriend as they are not his own.

Young boys and girls are treated very differently. Boys can run around unsupervised, while girls are expected to be quiet and helpful. Girls are carefully groomed and chaperoned. They are expected to be virgins at marriage and are vigilantly guarded against immoral conduct.

Little girls are encouraged to help their mothers and grandmothers, whether it is at home or in the marketplace.

ELDERS Grandparents almost always live with their families. They are held in high regard and viewed as wise. They are treated and spoken to with the utmost respect. However, grandparents rarely get very old, unless they come from a wealthy family, due to the lack of proper food and health care. Poverty and old age are rarely seen together and elders work as long as they are able. For them, there is no such thing as retirement.

LIFE CYCLE EVENTS

BIRTH Women accept pregnancies with joy even though they may not be able to afford any more children. Women in rural areas do not have hospitals to go to for childbirth, so birthing takes place at home with the help of the town's midwife, or simply other women in the family. Godparents are chosen and children are baptized in a Catholic church as soon as a priest is in town, which may not be until the next festival. If this is the case, many babies are baptized on the same day and a large town party may follow afterward.

A rural woman never retires. She contributes to the family's welfare all her life.

PUBERTY Children receive confirmation in a Catholic church when they are in their early teens. It is a time for all the relatives to celebrate. By this age, children have already taken on many responsibilities in the household or are working outside the house to earn money.

COURTSHIP AND MARRIAGE It is taboo for two teenagers to go on a date without a chaperone. If a date is arranged, sometimes the girl's whole family will go along. In this case, the boyfriend is expected to pay for the whole family. Because of widespread poverty, these dates do not occur often and marriages often take place after very little courtship.

Marriages, especially in rural areas, are often common-law because religious marriages are expensive and there may not be a residential priest. Some couples get a civil marriage, which is less expensive and makes it easier to get a divorce should things not work out. Middle- and upper-class couples usually have religious marriages with a formal engagement.

DEATH A Catholic funeral is very important in Honduras. The funeral service in church is followed by nine days of mourning at the deceased's home. This practice is repeated on the death anniversary.

A Bay Islands wedding party. After the ceremony, which takes place in a Catholic church, the bride's family usually holds an elaborate fiesta at their house with refreshments and dancing.

Above: **The ravages of slash-and-burn agriculture.**

Right: **Rural people cannot expect conveniences such as running water.**

Opposite: **One of the pleasures of living in rural towns is the *pulperia* ("pool-PEH-ree-ah"), or rural store, which is often also a place to socialize and catch up with the news.**

RURAL LIFESTYLES

For campesinos, or peasants, who live in the mountains, work is difficult and never done. But however busy or tired they are, they are always smiling and laughing at stories they share with one another. If they need to travel somewhere, such as the market, they go on foot, often spending the greatest part of their day walking.

A *campesina* ("kahm-pay-SEE-nah") wakes up at 5 a.m. and begins work in the kitchen. If she has daughters, they too will get up and help. Women spend the day making tortillas for their families. They boil, wash, and grind the corn to make coarse cornflour. They also bake bread, preserve fruit, wash clothes by hand, clean the house, and feed the chickens and cows. Mothers of infants tend to the babies, while the older girls spend much of their time looking after younger siblings.

Campesinos often wake up as early as 3 a.m. with their sons. They head out to the fields to plant, tend crops, or harvest. They use hoes, machetes, and digging sticks, and carry loads such as sacks of seed on their backs. Boys will receive their own plot of land to be responsible for at a young age—at 14 if they have been going to school.

Farming techniques traditionally involve the slash-and-burn method. Every two years families move to a new plot of land when the soil they have been farming has lost all its nutrients. They clear the land by slashing the growth down to the ground, then burning away the rest. Today, farmers are being taught soil conservation techniques such as terracing so that they will be able to farm one piece of land much longer.

Some campesinos also spend a part of their week squeezing sugarcane for juice to make sugar blocks to sell. Many campesinos are forced to find part-time work away from home to supplement their incomes as there is not enough land for all of them.

MARKETS Some families spend much of their time growing or making things to sell at the market. The families that do not live in a town with a market will load a small cart with their merchandise, which is then pulled by the family

cow. Hondurans may walk up to 20 miles (32 km) over pathless mountain ranges to get to a market. At the market, some women carry handmade baskets filled with flat breads on their heads as they look for buyers. Men and women work stalls where people come to barter over merchandise. They sell vegetables, fruit, bread, and chickens, as well as handmade straw hats, baskets, wooden statues of saints, vases, and toys.

HOUSING Families live in tiny rural towns, sometimes as small as a dozen dwellings clustered near a forlorn church, which is often the one-room schoolhouse as well. The homes are one- or two-room huts made from clay, adobe, or rough-hewn, unpainted boards and have palm leaf roofs and bare dirt floors. There is very rarely electricity, refrigeration, or running water. Water must be carried by mule or cow from the nearest streams, sometimes miles away.

On the road to the city of Comayagua, two sisters play at being grown-ups with a shawl and a basin. The road is graveled. In more rural areas, roads between villages, to markets, and between homes are often washed away after rain or hidden by clouds of dust during a dry spell.

URBAN LIFESTYLES

Compared to campesinos, urban residents live in comfort, although by Western standards, there are few conveniences available. Families still live together and everyone who is old enough to work adds to the family income. Very few Hondurans can afford a car or the expensive imported gasoline it runs on. Most people travel by taxi or bus—both are affordable and comfortable.

The men who work in the cities of Tegucigalpa, San Pedro Sula, Puerto Cortés, and La Ceiba are often skilled workers who went to a trade school, and a few to university. The head of the household, as well as any older sons, may be a mechanic, construction worker, furniture repairman, or an attendant at a filling station. Some men may own a small business with their brothers or cousins. After work, they may stop to have a few drinks with other men before returning home.

The women who work in the cities are often teachers, stenographers, secretaries, or domestic workers. Women are responsible for cleaning, laundry, and cooking in their own homes on top of working outside the home all day. A minority have refrigeration, electricity, and running water.

HOUSING A family in the city can usually afford a small home with an open patio and a red-tiled roof. Many people live in one-room apartments. Some homes have a small kitchen as well. The family traditionally gathers around the kitchen table at the end of the day to discuss events and share stories.

People are neatly dressed in the city.

EDUCATION

Public education is free and obligatory for every Honduran child from age 7 to 14, but not every child receives this benefit. Many students, especially in rural areas, go to school for grades one and two and then leave school to work and help earn a living for the family, usually by helping out on the farm. Nevertheless, this is a major improvement from before the education reforms of 1957 when there was no national education system, and education was the privilege of those wealthy enough to send their children to private institutions. In practice, this is still relatively true because of the shortage of schools and teachers, the poor wages and training of teachers, and the high cost of materials needed for public schools. The wealthy send their children to private schools where there are better-educated and better-paid teachers, as well as more money for school supplies.

Schoolgirls in a private school. Uniforms are the rule in the city whereas in the country children dress in their everyday clothes.

A RURAL SCHOOL DAY

Students wake as early as 3 a.m. to do chores before school—boys out on the farm, girls in the kitchen. They then walk to school, often a few miles. Classes start around 8 a.m. and go on until noon when it starts to get hot. When students arrive at school they usually get a free meal. This is very often the most nutritious meal they will eat all day. In primary (elementary) school a regular class will be taught Spanish vocabulary, and then students read or write a  story using the new vocabulary. Primary school students also learn farming techniques. Each class has its own plot of land where students grow beans and corn. Subjects in grades three to six include history, politics, mathematics, and science. At recess, girls sing and dance in large groups. Older boys play soccer. After school and the long walk home, children do more chores.

All schools are supported by the Catholic Church and catechism is taught in class. Schools in the cities are commonly divided into boys' and girls' schools.

There is typically only one teacher, usually female, for grades one and two. The teacher may have as many as 80 students in her classroom. Grades three to six also have one teacher per classroom. There are fewer students in the higher grades but they are still too many for one teacher to give significant time and attention to each individual.

HIGHER EDUCATION After completing grade six, a small number of students continue their education. Grades seven to nine are considered "college," or secondary school. Here students have a different teacher for each subject.

Grades 10 to 12 are called trade schools, or technical schools. Students who complete trade school may then become teachers, computer technicians, carpenters, and so on. Many women aspire to become teachers.

There are a few universities in Honduras, serving approximately 40,000 students. Hondurans go to university to become doctors, lawyers, professors, and engineers. More and more women go to university today.

The public education program includes billboards with visuals on how to avoid spreading disease.

LITERACY

Illiteracy rates vary depending on where Hondurans live. In rural settlements, especially in the western sections inhabited by Indians, more than 80% of the people cannot read and write. In the highlands near the capital and in the cities along the northern coast, illiteracy is much lower. The overall illiteracy rate is around 30%. The government is attempting to combat illiteracy, but because it is difficult to enforce the compulsory education law in remote areas, progress has been slow.

HEALTH AND WELFARE

The quality of health care and access to it vary depending on location and income levels. In rural areas access to trained medical personnel is limited, and in isolated regions there are almost no doctors. Rural inhabitants have to travel to Tegucigalpa or San Pedro Sula to receive quality medical care, but the cost of care and travel prevent many Hondurans from getting proper treatment.

The lack of medical care for the majority of Hondurans is apparent in their poor health. Poverty imposes restrictions on the food they eat, so malnutrition is widespread, causing 34% of children aged 2–5 to have stunted growth. The infant mortality rate is 42 per 1,000 live births and life expectancy is 68 years.

Most of the population lacks access to running water and sanitation facilities. Infectious and parasitic diseases are the leading causes of death. Gastroenteritis and tuberculosis are serious problems, as are influenza, malaria, typhoid, and pneumonia. Alcoholism and drug addiction are also common health problems. In the cities there has been a dramatic rise in

HIV infections that cause acquired immune deficiency syndrome (AIDS). The disease is spreading through intravenous drug use and prostitution. Population growth is still high, but women today are being taught birth control methods.

Hurricane Mitch brought health-related problems to the country in November 1998. Water contaminated by widespread death and destruction carried deadly diseases such as malaria and cholera. International relief brought in water purification machines and vaccinations against such diseases to help keep down the spread of fatal illnesses. Thousands suffered from respiratory illnesses, including pneumonia, after the rains.

HEALTH PERCEPTIONS Most Hondurans do not relate their health problems to their real causes, for example, to malnutrition or environmental hazards. When a state of affairs has existed for generations—there has not been a dramatic food shortage, for example, but the diet has been continually inadequate—people fail to make the connection between poor diet and poor health. Stunted children, infectious diseases, mental retardation, constant tiredness, and low productivity are viewed as normal because they have been occurring for centuries. Many Hondurans have never known what a healthy, nourished, comfortable life feels like.

CHOLERA

A cholera epidemic that originated in Peru hit Honduras in 1991. Cholera is a potentially fatal infectious disease that causes diarrhea, vomiting, and cramps. Since it is infectious, uncleanliness increases the spread of the disease. Because of the poor sanitation conditions in Honduras, officials were afraid cholera would spread rapidly throughout the country. The government quickly began an education campaign that stressed personal hygiene as a means of protection against cholera. By the middle of 1992, 100 cases of cholera were reported. This number may have been much higher had there been no education program.

RELIGION

THE HONDURAN CONSTITUTION guarantees religious freedom and the separation of church and state. Almost 90% of the population is Roman Catholic; the remaining groups are mostly Protestant. However, many Hondurans, especially in remote areas, have mixed their primary Christian religion with ancient Indian ceremonies, superstitions, and magic.

CATHOLICISM

The Spanish brought the Roman Catholic faith to Latin America over four and a half centuries ago. Many Hondurans are culturally Catholic rather than practicing Catholics. Catholic baptisms, first communions, weddings, and funerals are very important sacraments that celebrate milestones in people's lives.

Over the last three decades, however, the Catholic Church has been expanding the influence of Catholicism to enfold daily living and participation. The Church is also trying to recruit more Honduran-born clerics. Of the almost 300 priests working in Honduras, only about 70 are native Hondurans.

Above: **Vendors arrange their goods near the 16th century Iglesia de Los Dolores (Church of Sufferers), in Tegucigalpa.**

Opposite: **A somewhat martial looking stained glass image of the Virgin Mary, with the Honduran coat of arms at top left.**

INCREASING RELIGIOUS ACTIVITIES In the 1950s and 1960s, priests and nuns were sent to Honduras from around the world to build churches and evangelize in order to increase Catholic membership and activities. These missionaries found a country of devout people who had as much belief in superstition and magic as in church dogma.

The Catholic Church reached out to the rural areas where poverty and illiteracy were widespread. It tackled these socioeconomic problems by

día mundial del Sida.
todo enfermo es tu hermano

The Catholic Church in Honduras has a public education program for issues such as AIDS.

introducing literacy and social service programs. With the creation of church groups such as the Christian Movement for Justice, the Catholic Church has taken on an important social role in Honduran society. Catholic schools receive government subsidies, and religious instruction is a part of the public school curriculum.

THE CULT OF THE SAINTS Hondurans believe in the power of Catholic saints. In each Catholic home, there is a picture or statue of a particular saint, very often the Virgin Mary. People pray to the saints for intervention or protection in their lives. Other popular saints are ones that are believed to offer protection on given occasions, such as traveling, or that bless a particular situation, such as the health of infants and children. Hondurans also make pilgrimages to pray to certain saints during particular festivals or occasions. Some people promise to make a pilgrimage if a certain prayer is answered. Pilgrimages to the Basilica of the Virgin of Suyapa near Tegucigalpa and to Esquipulas in Guatemala are made faithfully.

SACRAMENTS The Catholic religion begins playing a role in the life of a Honduran with baptism. If a small town does not have its own priest, it is customary to wait for a fiesta when a priest will come to celebrate the festival and, at that time, perform all the town's baptisms at once. A fiesta usually follows a baptism and the whole extended family attend.

After a Catholic marriage ceremony, where there is an exchange of rings and vows, a fiesta is held in the home of either the bride or groom's parents—usually at the house of whomever is wealthier. After food and drink at the house, the celebration shifts to a larger hall for a dance if the budget allows.

Catholic funerals are absolutely traditional within Catholic families. Immediately after death, the family holds a *novena* ("noh-VAY-nah"), or nine nights of prayer in front of the saint's altar at home. Novenas are also often held six months after the death and on its first anniversary. Close friends and family are invited to novenas.

PROTESTANTISM

Evangélicos ("eh-van-HAY-lee-kohs") are Protestant groups that have emerged as important religious forces since the 1980s. They are also sponsors of many social service programs that receive much of their

Homes of Catholic families in Honduras have an altar for religious images, which is usually decorated with flowers.

79

A church in Danlí, near the Nicaraguan border, typically in the Spanish-colonial style.

funding from the United States. Few Hondurans who profess to be evangelicals belong to the mainstream Protestant denominations, such as Lutheran. Today the largest evangelical churches in the country are the Methodists, the Southern Baptists, the Central American Mission, and the charismatic Pentecostal denomination, the Assemblies of God. The largest population of Protestants are the English-speaking inhabitants of the Bay Islands. This geographical religious split is due to the fact that the British were the main influence in the Bay Islands, not the Roman Catholic Spanish who ruled the mainland.

PLACES OF WORSHIP

Places of worship in Honduras include Catholic and Protestant churches that vary from extravagant ornate basilicas, presided over by a bishop, to meager thatched-roof buildings in small towns, with no priest at all. Paintings and statues of saints decorate the Roman Catholic churches regardless of the town's wealth.

Catholics may go to church to pray to a saint different from the one they venerate in their own home. Masses are held on Sundays, mostly in Spanish, but there are services in English in the larger cities.

The Protestant evangelical churches are newer and simpler in style, reflecting their belief that the church is made of people, not walls. English services are more common in evangelical churches due to the British and American influence in the spread of the Protestant faith.

OTHER RELIGIONS

The immigrant population accounts for the presence of other religions in Tegucigalpa and San Pedro Sula. They include Judaism (Jews), Church of Jesus Christ of Latter-day Saints (Mormons), and Mennonite Protestantism. There are also a few indigenous tribal religions, as well as some African religious traditions practiced by the Black Carib on the north coast.

Singing in an evangelical church.

Selling traditional medicines is good business, whether on sidewalks or in public buses.

Many indigenous groups have their own religions that exist alongside Christianity and include elements of African and Indian animism and ancestor worship.

FOLK BELIEFS

Some indigenous customs and traits have survived in the otherwise Catholic and Protestant communities. Hondurans today are not as superstitious as their parents and grandparents, but many Hondurans believe that certain people have the power to do good or evil based on magic and psychic or supernatural forces. In remote areas people consult priests for advice on marriage, feuds with neighbors, and spells of bad luck, much like their ancestors consulted the medicine man.

FOLK MEDICINE Many Hondurans have very limited access to modern Western medicine. Therefore, folk medicine plays a major role, especially for the poor and those who live in remote regions. Towns usually have a spiritual person who is known for handling illnesses, reminiscent of a traditional medicine man, who is called upon to prescribe herbs and say prayers. Sometimes this person is a midwife, and occasionally it is the storekeeper who sells traditional cures.

The Basilica of the Virgin of Suyapa is the site of pilgrimage throughout the year, and especially on the saint's day, February 3.

Massage and purging are common practices to rid a person of his or her sickness. Many Hondurans also believe foods belong to the "hot" or "cold" category and that one or the other should be avoided or prescribed to cure common ailments. "Hot" foods such as coffee, oranges, and beef are believed to irritate the digestive system. "Cold foods" like coconuts, bananas, salt, and most kinds of seafood are believed to cause stomach upset. Herbs are also divided into hot or cold and are used to treat illnesses.

THE VIRGIN OF SUYAPA Outside Tegucigalpa, in a place called Suyapa, is one of Central America's most impressive religious shrines, the Basilica of the Virgin of Suyapa, the patron saint of Honduras and all Central America. The small 18th century statue of the Virgin is believed to have miraculous healing powers. The figurine is honored inside the massive basilica, which is decorated with magnificent stained glass windows and a marble altar with bronze and gold designs. The Fair of the Virgin of Suyapa takes place every year throughout Honduras from February third to 10th. This fair is one of Honduras' most important holidays.

LANGUAGE

THE OFFICIAL LANGUAGE of Honduras is Spanish. English, however, is the primary language of the Bay Islands. English is also spoken to some extent in the large cities. A few indigenous languages are still spoken today in remote regions.

SPANISH

Just as the colonial Spanish explorers brought their customs, they also brought their language. However, like most Latin American countries, Hondurans do not speak Castilian Spanish, the official standard Spanish of Spain that originated in the Castile region.

All Spanish has gender-specific forms of nouns and adjectives—masculine nouns end in "o," feminine nouns end in "a," and the adjectives used to describe the nouns agree with its gender. For example, a little boy

Left and opposite: **Official signs and most newspapers in Honduras are in Spanish.**

is *el chiquito muchacho* ("el chee-KEE-toh moo-CHAH-choh"). A little girl is *la chiquita muchacha* ("lah chee-KEE-tah moo-CHAH-chah").

Spanish also has formal and informal forms of words. The familiar form of you is *tú*, the more formal form is *vos*. In daily conversations between Hondurans who know each other well the familiar tú is used.

Hondurans, like other Latin Americans, often use diminutives to soften what they are saying, making speech more familiar, affectionate, and compassionate. For instance, instead of saying *momento* ("moh-MAIN-toh"), which means "a moment," they will say *momentito* ("moh-main-TEE-toh"), which makes "Just a minute!" sound a little more apologetic.

OTHER LANGUAGES

English is the main language spoken in the Bay Islands. Black and white immigrants from the Antilles, the main group of islands in the West Indies, and from British Honduras (today known as Belize) settled the Bay Islands near the end of the colonial period and have kept their island version of English alive. Arabic is also spoken on the Bay Islands by immigrants from the Middle East.

Indigenous languages are mostly isolated within remote Indian communities. However, there are various slang words in the Spanish speaking Ladino culture that are Indian in origin. There are also many names of places, towns, and streets that are derived from Nahuatl, the language of the Mexican allies of the Spanish conquerors. The Pipil people (related to the Chortí Indians) near the El Salvadoran border still speak a language related to Nahuatl. The large indigenous group, the Lencas, speak various dialects of their language, although Spanish is being adopted by their communities today. The Miskito Indians continue to speak a language similar to the Miskito of South America.

Opposite: **Lencas speak a number of Lenca dialects, but they also speak Spanish to communicate with other Hondurans.**

HONDURAS' UNWRITTEN LANGUAGES

Some indigenous languages in Honduras do not have a written alphabet or text. The Pech of northeastern Honduras are an example. In an attempt to keep the Pech language alive in the midst of the predominantly Spanish Honduran culture, some linguists have been working in recent years to develop a written language. First these linguists, together with Pech teachers, had to create an alphabet.

The Pech have a very complicated vowel system—long vowels, short vowels, nasal vowels, glottal vowels, and vowels with an aspiration after them. But most complicated of all, Pech have high and low tones that are very difficult to represent in writing.

Many people have collaborated on this project and the first two books in Pech were printed in 1996 using the new alphabet. A Spanish-Pech dictionary and books for second graders are also being prepared for publication. Although the Ministry of Education has not set an official schedule to launch the Pech language program in schools, it will soon be taught in every Pech school. The Pech have expressed their gratitude for the effort to preserve their language by naming one of their schools after a Honduran linguist who worked on the project.

Chickens have a strong presence in Honduran culture and language. Not surprisingly, therefore, they are popular in crafts. One finds carved wooden chickens, ceramic chickens, chickens painted on vases, and hollow chicken coin banks.

NONVERBAL COMMUNICATION

Hondurans use their hands and arms a great deal when speaking, especially when they are passionate about their subject. In general, they gesticulate more than Americans do.

In the city, it is expected that, when greeting one another, women kiss women, men kiss women, and women kiss men. Men who are meeting one another for the first time shake hands and say their names loudly at the same time, a practice that makes it difficult to hear the other person's name.

COMMON EXPRESSIONS

Terms of endearment are most important in Honduras because the people are very friendly, warm, and caring. Adults speaking to children will often use the term *niño* ("NEE-nyo") or *niña* ("NEE-nya") which means child. When Hondurans want to use a term of endearment for a beloved sister or female cousin or friend, they use the term *tita* ("TEE-tah"). When speaking to a brother or male cousin or friend, they use the term *tito* ("TEE-toh"). When children want to use a term of endearment for either their mother or grandmother, they say *mamita* ("mah-MEE-tah"). And when speaking to their father or grandfather, they say *papita*. Otherwise, children refer to parents as mom and pa, or *mamá* ("mah-MAH") and *papá* ("pah-PAH"). But they are careful not to put the accent in the wrong place for *papa*, because "PAH-pah" means potato or Pope!

Chickens and roosters have come to play a large role in Honduran folktales and expressions. They use the term "henpecked" in an unusual context—from a joke about a Honduran president's parrot that was pecked free of its feathers by chickens in a henhouse. They also use the expression "*este es mi gallo*" ("EHS-teh ehs mee GAH-yo"), which means

"this is my rooster." This expression was originally used by Hondurans who had bet on a winning rooster during a cockfight, but today it is used to mean something along the lines of "this is mine and it is the best!"

Hondurans of different ethnic backgrounds have a common language base in Spanish.

CORRECT COMMUNICATION

IN BUSINESS Business letters in Honduras often begin with an elaborate, fervent, positive greeting, even if the rest of the letter is terribly negative. For example, a common opening sentence would be: "I hope that this letter finds you in the best of health and that all of your family and loved ones are healthy and prospering." A short, brisk letter would appear rude and altogether unkind to a Honduran.

AT A MEETING Hondurans are more verbal than many cultures. Instead of quietly slinking late into a meeting that has started, the latecomer must call out a greeting. Hondurans forgive lateness, but not a person who forgets to say *Buenos dias!* ("BWAY-nos DEE-as")

BEFORE A MEAL When sitting down with someone who is eating, whether he or she is a relative or a business acquaintance, well-mannered Hondurans sit down and say "*Buen provecho*" ("boo-en pro-VEH-cho"), which means "much good may it do you!"

SPOKEN AND WRITTEN LANGUAGE

Spanish uses a Roman alphabet, as English does. There are, however, a few differences. In Spanish *ch*, *ll*, and *rr* are considered to be single, separate letters. When speaking, *rr* is rolled stronger and longer than a single *r*. The double *l* (*ll*), on the other hand, sounds more like a *y*. The letter *ñ* is also a separate letter. *B* and *v* have the same sound. *K* and *w* do not exist in the Spanish language, but these letters are found in foreign words that have been adopted by Hondurans.

Spanish is written in the Roman alphabet and some of the words are close enough to English for an English-language speaker to understand.

NAMES AND TITLES

Popular first names in Honduras today for girls are Suyapa (named after the Virgin of Suyapa), Jessica, and Maria. Popular names for boys are Mario, Carlos, José, and Antonio.

Hondurans follow the Spanish custom of forming a double surname by taking the family surname of each parent. For instance a young woman by the name of Teresa Vásquez González has two surnames—González from her mother, Vásquez from her father. Formally she is known as Señorita Vásquez. If she marries a man by the name of Rodrígez Velez Carboñera, she takes his father's surname, losing her own mother's— Teresa Vásquez de Carboñera or Señora de Carboñera.

For men, after the first mention of their full name, they are called by their father's surname, for instance, Oscar Calderón Hernández is referred to as Señor Oscar Calderón. However, some men prefer to use both surnames.

TITLES Titles are also important in Honduras. Becoming a teacher, lawyer, professor, engineer, architect, or doctor takes a lot of effort and determination. Therefore, Hondurans believe a professional person has earned his or her title and should be spoken of with it. Just as Americans say Doctor Jones, Hondurans say Doctor Moreno, as well as Teacher Avila, Professor Martinez, and Attorney Nuñez.

Respect for elders is extremely important for Hondurans. A male adult is *Señor* and a female adult who is married is *Señora*. Someone who is a very well respected member of a community earns the higher title of *Don* for a man, and *Doña* for a woman. If these terms were not used, a person would be very insulted. There is a difference between the big cities and the small villages. In cities it is common to always use the terms Señor or Señora. In the villages Don and Doña are the most acceptable titles when speaking with respect.

Hondurans say buenos dias *in greeting when they meet and* buenos noches *("BWAY-nos NAW-chez") when they part. To pass each other without a greeting would be considered very rude.*

GREETINGS

When greeting one another, women often embrace and sometimes give each other one kiss on the cheek. Men shake hands, but would never embrace. Men do hug children when they are young. Women often hug their own children, even when they are grown up, and will hug other women's children too. In the cities, a man may sometimes embrace a woman who is not related to him and kiss her on the cheek. However, in rural areas a man would never kiss a woman who was not his wife. Such an action is considered taboo.

ARTS

HONDURAS HAS A RICH COMBINATION of Ladino and indigenous traditions. Dance, painting, poetry, and folk crafts draw from traditional Honduran beliefs and folklore as well as modern influences. The promotion of fine arts has been intensified recently thanks to public and private institutions that organize exhibitions and contests where new and old generations of artists can come together.

PERFORMING ARTS

DANCE Dancing is a vital part of Honduran culture. Each department has its own traditional dance. Boys and girls learn this and perform it at festivals. Almost every girl has a traditional dress, always bright and colorful, to be worn on these occasions. Women's skirts are full and the blouses have ruffled collars and sleeves. Men wear full pants and ruffled shirts as well. Many official folk dance groups exist in the cities, whose members are older students. Competitions are intense and attract a large audience. Groups from universities are considered professional. Young girls look up to these university dancers and aspire to be as talented when they are older.

Above: **A Garifuna boy dances the *mascaro*, or mask, dance in La Ceiba.**

Opposite: **A Chortí woman weaves a mat. Folk crafts are a living part of the indigenous culture.**

There are hundreds of well-known traditional dances in Honduras. The *maladio wanaragua* ("mah-LAH-dee-oh wah-nah-RAH-gwah") is a mask dance that represents the fight of the Garifuna against England. The *sique* ("seek") dance has its origins in the dances of the early Indians. Another popular dance on the north coast is the *mascaro* ("mas-KAH-roh"), which shows strong African influences. Hondurans also love common Latin American dances such as the samba and salsa.

The Garifuna (Black Carib) of the northern coast have a very important dance that originated on the island of St. Vincent in the Caribbean. The *punta* ("POOHN-tah") is traditionally danced when a relative dies so that the spirit stays on earth. It is also said to be a dance invoking fertility. However, the influence of the punta has stretched far beyond traditional boundaries. Young girls learn the dance from older sisters. Teenagers and young adults do the punta in discos around the country. And people come from all around to watch the original punta dancers, the Garifuna, in the city of La Ceiba.

MUSIC It is common to hear the music of a *marimba* ("mah-RIM-bah") band in full swing at any hour of the day or night. Like all Latin Americans, Hondurans love music. They love boleros or anything with a cha-cha rhythm and a lively beat. Honduran music has developed into varied rhythms and styles recalling the religious and folkloric traits of each ethnic group. There are not very many professional musical groups aside from marimba bands.

A musician plays on turtleshells in Trujillo, on the northern coast. Other favorite instruments in Honduras are the guitar, accordion, and conch shells.

PUNTA

The drums beat loudly as Hondurans gather around, and the dancers begin to clap and stomp their feet. Faces are illuminated by firelight. Wide smiles and bright eyes reflect enthusiasm. A young dancer darts out into the middle of the circle formed by the crowd and begins to dance with swinging hips and small steps toward the drummers. A moment passes, then a young man joins her in the circle. He dances before her while the audience sends out cheers of encouragement. This is punta.

MARIMBA

The marimba consists of tuned wooden keys, like a xylophone, attached to resonators that hang below the keys to amplify the sound. Common resonators are gourds or wooden bell shapes. The marimba produces sound when its keys are struck with a rubber-tipped stick.

There are three kinds of marimba. The simplest is the *marimba con tecomates* ("te-koh-MAH-tez"), which is worn by one person over the shoulders and held with straps to place the instrument horizontally across the waist. It is associated with rural ceremonial events.

The *marimba doble* is really two instruments played as one by seven men. It is set up on the ground with removable legs. It is associated with urban centers and commercial, professional activities, and is found at large festivals.

The *marimba sencilla* ("sen-SI-lah") is a single instrument played by three men. It also stands on the ground. Because it is smaller than the doble and bigger than the con tecomates, the sencilla is played at a wide range of events, in rural and urban areas.

There are a few classical music groups and a symphony orchestra. Two large annual music festivals bring both symphony and folk composers and performers together to celebrate music.

The marimba is the best-loved and most representative instrument of Central America. It was introduced to Honduras by African slaves but its origin can be traced from Southeast Asia, through Africa, to Latin America. Modern adaptations and improvements of the instrument are attributed to Central America. A *marimbero* ("mah-rim-BAY-roh") is a person who plays the marimba. There are various forms of the marimba, but usually a whole ensemble, not just one person, plays a large, multifaceted one. Members of a marimba ensemble are usually men from the same family. There are a few women ensembles today, but a mixed gender group would be quite unusual. Children's groups in schools are either a boys' group or a girls'.

Other popular musical instruments are the *caramba* ("cah-RAHM-bah"), a string instrument found mostly in rural areas, and acoustic and classical guitars.

Examples of Baroque, Renaissance, and Moorish architecture can be found in Honduras, but these are in the minority. Spanish-colonial architecture and the Mayan influence are more evident.

OTHER PERFORMING ARTS Honduras does not have a large theater tradition. There are small drama groups, and towns and villages have their own small groups that dramatize religious stories during festivals.

Traditional puppet shows are performed in some towns and cities and are enjoyed by both children and adults.

ARCHITECTURE

The ornate temples and elaborately constructed buildings and pyramids of the ancient Maya influence how modern Hondurans build and decorate their buildings. Tegucigalpa's Concordia Park is dedicated to the memory of the Maya with a miniature Mayan temple that shows their distinctive and elaborate ornamentation. In the larger cities of Honduras, intricate carvings and designs of the pre-Columbian era have been artfully integrated into Spanish-colonial architecture.

The colonial influence—large, arched doorways and domes atop churches—is seen in many buildings throughout the country. These old-style buildings stand in stark contrast to the skyscrapers in Tegucigalpa and San Pedro Sula that use the latest building materials, technology, and design. They house mostly government offices and big, often foreign, businesses. In front of these modern buildings there are still the quaint shaded canteens where Hondurans feel most comfortable.

VISUAL ARTS

PAINTING constitutes the strongest base in the modern artistic development of Honduras. Most people believe the fine arts in Honduras was in fact founded by José Miguel Gomez in the 18th century with his religious paintings. Although they show a European influence, they have a distinctly Honduran style. Contemporary Honduran painting began in the 1920s.

Today, self-taught painters all over the country are dedicated to depicting beautiful, primitive Honduran landscapes and modest towns.

One of the best-known painters in Honduras is Arturo López Rodezno. To train new artists he founded the National School of Arts and Crafts. His paintings and school have influenced artists in Honduras and from all over the world. José Antonio Valázquez is famous for his paintings depicting life in his village, San Antonio de Oriente, which provide the world a window into Honduran life. His most famous painting is of Tegucigalpa's main square with the statue of Francisco Morazán.

A favorite painter in Honduras is Dilber Padilla, who is known for his use of vibrant colors, especially red. His work is considered enigmatic, suggestive, impressionistic, and contemporary. He claims to be inspired by Van Gogh and a contemporary Guatemalan artist, Elman Rojas. Cruz Bermudez is a Garifuna painter who loves nature and paints endangered species to publicize their dilemma.

A popular theme in painting is the "Rain of Fish" showing hundreds of fish raining down from the sky. It is based on a Honduran phenomenon where villagers in the department of Yoro woke up after a June thunderstorm to find the ground strewn with fish! One explanation of the strange event is that these fish followed a low pressure system in from the sea near the end of their lifespan. They leapt ashore during the storm and suffocated. It is not hard to imagine why this fantastic event has inspired so many painters over the years.

Carnaval, a vivid painting by Arturo López Rodezno.

JOSÉ ANTONIO VALÁZQUEZ (1906–83)

Valázquez is probably the most celebrated Honduran painter. He is internationally known for his primitivist paintings of his village of San Antonio de Oriente, a 16th century mining center high in the mountains southeast of Tegucigalpa. Valázquez was a barber by profession without any formal artistic training. He began to paint in 1927 and moved to San Antonio de Oriente in 1930 where he was the town barber and telegraph operator. His unique primitive paintings reflect the humble tranquility of that village where he spent most of the next 30 years of his life.

Valázquez and his paintings were not discovered until 1943 when he met Dr. Wilson Popenoe, director of the Agricultural School at El Zamorano. Popenoe hired him as a barber at his school but encouraged him to market his paintings in Tegucigalpa where they sold for low prices. In 1954 Popenoe organized an exhibition of Valázquez's paintings in Washington D.C., where the artist gained international acclaim. In 1955 he was given the National Prize for Art, Honduras' most important award for art. He was also elected mayor of San Antonio de Oriente. Valázquez's son and grandson have carried on his primitivist traditions. Valázquez's work is on permanent display in many of Tegucigalpa's finest hotels and galleries.

SCULPTURE has developed a high social and aesthetic value in recent years in Honduras and sculptors work with bronze, wood, and ceramics. Modern sculptors are obviously influenced by folk crafts.

LITERATURE

Authors in Honduras traditionally started their careers as newspaper journalists because there were not many local magazines. Honduran newspapers typically print poems, essays, and short stories so budding writers can publish and polish their work in the papers and at the same time develop a readership. An author who has a following would then approach a publisher with a collection of poems, essays, or short stories, or a novel and may pay to have the work published. Because of the cost

JOSÉ TRINIDAD REYES (1797–1855)

Reyes, known as the Father of Higher Education in Honduras, was multitalented—a playwright, poet, politician, and educator. He was born in Tegucigalpa to poor parents, and his humble origins prevented him from furthering his studies in Comayagua. He went to Nicaragua where he graduated with a degree in philosophy, theology, and canon law. In 1822 he was ordained a Catholic priest. In 1840 he was named bishop of Honduras by Rome, but political intrigue prevented him from assuming this position.  Reyes was opposed to the president of Honduras, Zelaya y Ayes, so Ayes told Rome that Reyes had died! Under a new president, Reyes turned a literary academy into the first university in Honduras, Universidad Nacional Autonóma de Honduras. He was named its first rector. In 1846 Reyes was named Poet Laureate of Honduras. He is known for bringing the first printing press to Honduras and the first piano to Tegucigalpa. Reyes' book on physics was a textbook in Honduras for many years.

LUCILA GAMERO DE MEDINA (1873–1964)

Medina wrote the first Honduran novel to be published. She was an amazing woman for her time—a physician, an essayist, a feminist, and a novelist. She published many novels during her long and productive life. Her first two novels, *Amalia Montiel* and *Adriana y Margarita,* were published in Tegucigalpa in 1893 when she was only 20 years old. They are still read today. Her most famous novel is *Blanca Olmedo* (1903), a controversial attack on the Catholic clergy. Medina was an intelligent, talented, and ambitious woman whom Honduran women admire and try to emulate.

involved in becoming a published writer, authors in Honduras are often wealthy and not representative of the common Honduran.

There are few young adult and children's books written in Honduras, as such literature is not very profitable yet. Children's books come from Spain, Mexico, Argentina, and the United States. Most stories are Spanish versions of well-known tales such as *The Tortoise and the Hare*.

Several Hondurans have made important contributions to literature. José Cecilio del Valle, the political leader who framed the nation's declaration of independence in the colonial period, was a prominent scholar and newspaper publisher. Poet-historian Rafael Heliodoro Valle, who died in 1959, is also well-known. Among writers recognized outside Honduras are José Trinidad Reyes and Ramón Rosa from the earlier years and Juan Molina, Marcos Reyes, and Rafael H. Valle in modern times.

A young woman of the department of Olancho northeast of Tegucigalpa paints her house in muted, earthy tones.

FOLK ARTS AND CRAFTS

Remnants of Pre-Columbian Mayan crafts can be found in Honduras. More common are the contemporary folk crafts sold in markets scattered around Honduras. Many Hondurans are skilled in folk crafts and can usually earn some extra money for their families by selling their products. The wealthy as well as the poor make these traditional crafts as presents for birthdays, baptisms, weddings, and Christmas. Certain areas are renowned for a particular craft such as superb woodcarvings or fine jewelry.

Common Honduran crafts include small wooden or clay hollow animals such as chickens, pigs, dogs, macaws, and other birds. These are painted in many bright colors with intricate designs. A version of this craft has a coin slot in the side to make it into a coin-bank. In order to get the coins out, children have to smash the animal.

Vases are also popular. Black vases of different sizes are painted with tiny, intricate flowers and then filled with large, bright, tropical flowers. Other crafts seen in the markets are handwoven grass bread baskets and laundry baskets. The Garifuna weave a special sleeping mat from a long, slender grass called *nea* ("NEH-ah").

Over the span of many generations, woodcarving has been honed to a fine art, especially in the town of Valle de Angeles near Tegucigalpa, which is dedicated to crafts. Furniture is one of their specialties. Furniture carved in Valle de Angeles is characterized by its intricate, deep-relief carvings of the village's streets, flowers, and marine life. These craftsmen make coffee tables, mirror frames, and trunks of all shapes and sizes. The wood they use is from the beautiful native cedar tree. Trunks are especially popular. Each takes about a week to make.

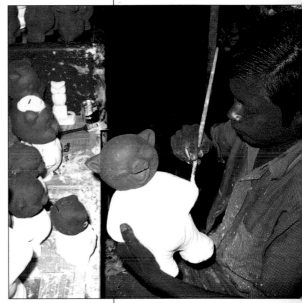

A boy paints earthenware piggy-banks, which will be sold in marketplaces throughout Honduras.

GUAMILITO

Guamilito Market in downtown San Pedro Sula is one of the wonderful large city markets of Honduras. It is an excellent place to buy and sell handicrafts from all over Honduras. The most popular items are handwoven hats, large wicker baskets, woodcarvings, miniature paintings, leather goods such as belts, clothing, shoes, and bags, and colorful cotton hammocks. Hand-painted feathers and seeds with minute landscapes are delicate and detailed, as are the intricately carved relief landscapes on cedar. Most artists come to the market themselves to sell their crafts and often bring their whole family. The market is awash with bright tropical colors of crafts, flowers, and fruit.

LEISURE

UNLESS THEY ARE WEALTHY, Hondurans do not have a lot of time or money for leisure activities. The time for the leisure activities they do participate in, such as soccer, dancing, and singing is highly valued. Most Hondurans spend their leisure time with their families.

SPORTS

Young boys play the most sports. At school there is time at recess to be physically active with other boys. Sometimes on Sundays time will be taken for a game or two.

SOCCER is by far the most popular sport for boys and men to play, as well as to watch. Association football, as soccer is called in Honduras, is the national sport. In order to become a hero, one need only be an outstanding soccer player. Honduran boys can enjoy a fast game of soccer, while claiming it is too hot to work in the fields. Hondurans passionately follow the sport at the local, national, and international levels. Emotions often run high. Most Hondurans listen to big games on the radio, as most people do not have television. Almost every town has a soccer team.

OTHER SPORTS Basketball is quickly becoming popular in the cities of Honduras. Private schools have teams for basketball, volleyball, tennis, and baseball. Golf is played near the bigger cities by wealthy men. Sports for women have not been very popular in Honduras.

Sport fishing is also popular among the wealthy. Along the Caribbean coast and on the Bay Islands people come from all over to fish for tuna, barracuda, shark, blue and white marlin, sailfish, wahoo, mahi-mahi, grouper, kingfish, and red snapper.

Above and opposite: **Soccer is *the* sport in Honduras, whether it is kicking a ball around in Yoro or taking a penalty kick on Roatán Island.**

Boys playing checkers after class.

People also come from all over the world to dive and snorkel at the coral reefs of the Bay Islands. The water is warm and clear and underwater visibility is very good. It is mostly Honduras' wealthier inhabitants that take part in these activities.

LEISURE ACTIVITIES

Dance and song have long been very important to Hondurans. Young girls usually learn the traditional dance of their department, as well as the popular punta dance at a young age. Many city girls go on to take ballet or other forms of dance classes. In the absence of sports activities for the majority of girls, dancing gives girls the physical activity and "team" fun they need.

There are many songs about Honduras that boys and girls alike learn when they are very young. The national anthem is popular, and Honduran children and adults feel proud when they sing it. Girls will often sing and dance during recess and after school if they have any free time.

While the boys are playing soccer, young girls play outdoors with their friends and cousins. They enjoy a game called *landa* ("LAHN-dah") where a group of them stand in a circle and push each other around, catching each other's fall. Older girls spend the evening with friends. On weekends dancing at the local disco is the most popular activity. Even small towns have discos where teenagers dance the punta and other popular Latin American dances, as well as to popular music from the United States.

People also enjoy going to the beach, especially during national holidays. Hondurans swim, sunbathe, picnic, and surf whenever they can. Other activities that may challenge the mind and pass away the hours are cards, chess, and checkers. But most often in the evenings, Hondurans simply spend time with their families discussing the day's events.

As in most large cities of the world, people who have the time, interest, and a little extra money take classes in almost anything. Tegucigalpa offers classes in acting, guitar, drawing, painting, chess, and many forms of dance. Tegucigalpa even has a cigar club.

Hondurans have a wide choice of beaches, particularly in the north, so picnicking near the sea is a favorite leisure activity.

The radio is the most common way to get the news in Honduras, since not everyone is literate and few have television. People also listen to stories and soccer games on the radio in the evenings.

STORYTELLING

Storytelling is a popular activity among Honduran families with grandparents and other elders passing their evenings telling children folktales. Dramatic storytelling is an event during festivals that the celebrants thoroughly enjoy. Stories include tales about the Spanish colonials, animals like horses and chickens, spirits, and thieves. Some stories are intended to teach moral lessons. Others are told in the form of jokes.

One of the most popular characters in Honduran oral literature is the *duende* ("DWEHN-deh"), a short man who lives in the woods. Some of the stories about duende are told by parents to frighten children so that they will not stray into the woods. The most famous theme for duende stories is his attempt to get young girls to fall in love with him.

ROOSTERS IN HONDURAN CULTURE

Chickens show up all over Honduran culture. Chickens are kept not just for eggs and meat, but also as pets.

A popular leisure activity is cockfighting. In the Ladino culture cockfighting is an acceptable form of sport, and cockfights are considered an essential part of many patron saint festivals. Men who own fighting roosters carry them to distant villages to cockfighting events.

RADIO AND TELEVISION

The radio is still a popular source of entertainment because few towns, let alone homes, have television. Television is more popular in the cities, but not abundant. Television programs include Western movies, cartoons, and game shows from the United States translated into Spanish and programs from Mexico, including soap operas.

DUENDE STORY

Duende stories are popular with young girls. This is a favorite in many Ladino villages:

Years ago in a little village, there was a group of beautiful young women. As the day of St. Anthony, the patron saint of the area, came near, these women decided to go into the woods in search of firewood for the upcoming celebrations. On their way they talked happily about the fair. After collecting wood, each gathered up her bundle and began to haul it back to the village.

Suddenly the youngest woman, who was trailing at the back of the group, saw a beautiful flower. She put down her bundle to pick the flower. As soon as she picked it, another one bloomed a few steps away. Each time she picked one, an even prettier one appeared up ahead. She kept collecting flowers until she realized she was lost. She could only see a wonderful world of flowers and hear a faint whistling. As she saw the most beautiful flower yet, she thought of her patron saint and exclaimed, "This is the most beautiful flower I have seen in my entire life. I will cut it and put it on the altar of blessed St. Anthony." As soon as she said these words, all the flowers disappeared. At that instant her companions, who had been looking for her, found her, and she told them what had happened.

Since that day, every time the festival of St. Anthony draws near, the people of the village hear melodic whistles from an unseen person and smell the aroma of sweet flowers. The people say the duende must have wanted to carry the young woman away but failed because she was protected by her patron saint. Every year he comes back again, looking for a beautiful woman to carry away and keep him company.

CHICKEN FOLKTALE

Hondurans are always on the lookout to protect their chickens from deadly encounters with hawks and cats. This story is about chickens and a hawk:

Among the Garifuna, men and boys fish and women and girls take care of the fields and animals. A mother complained to her son that a hawk was carrying off the family's chickens one by one. She asked him to stay home to help her watch over the chickens. The boy did not want to miss any fishing, but he did want to help his mother. So he tied all of the chickens together by their feet before he left to go fishing, thinking it would keep the hawk from being able to carry them away. Instead, the hawk was able to steal all of the chickens at once rather than one by one.

There are many children's songs about chickens, crafts that use the chicken motif, folktales involving chickens, and even chicken dances. One children's song tells about the day the red rooster overslept. No one, not even the sun, got up that day because no one heard the rooster's "kirikiri!"

FESTIVALS

HONDURAS HAS MANY NATIONAL HOLIDAYS, both religious and secular. It is a country that knows how to forget its poverty on occasion and celebrate. For official national holidays, employers are required to pay employees for the days off, even if it is a Sunday. Most festivals are celebrated as street fairs with singing and traditional dancing. Extended families get together to spend the fiesta together.

Opposite: **A Carnaval queen and her "king" on a float down a main street in La Ceiba.**

CELEBRATING SECULAR HOLIDAYS

Many of the secular festival days are celebrated in a small way in the community. There are many days that honor people or ideas. Language Day is celebrated mostly in school by students participating in competitions. Teachers choose the students with the best vocabulary, spelling, and writing. On Teachers' Day, students bring their teachers flowers, candy,

NATIONAL SECULAR HOLIDAYS AND FESTIVALS

January 1	New Year's Day	July 14	Democracy Day
March 19	Father's Day	July 20	Lempira Day
April 14	Day of the Americas	August 3	Ethnic Day
April 23	Language Day	September 10	Children's Day
May 1	Labor Day	September 15	Independence Day
2nd Sunday in May	Mother's Day	September 17	Teachers' Day
		September 28	Declaration of Independence
May 30	Tree Day	October 2	Discovery of Honduras
June 5	Environment Day	October 3	Francisco Morazán's Birthday
June 9	José Trinidad Cabañas Day	October 21	Armed Forces Day
		October 24	National Union's Day
June 12	Students' Day	November 18	Nationality Day
June 14	Flag Day	November 22	José Cecilio de Valle Day

A costume pageant provides excitement for both the participants and the spectators on Children's Day.

or fruit. Tree Day celebrates the trees that provide our world with oxygen whereas Environment Day honors trees, plants, animals, and water. Labor Day is honored by Hondurans staging peaceful protests in the cities. Many campesinos will take the long bus ride or walk to Tegucigalpa on this day to celebrate the power of laborers in Honduras.

New Year's Eve is a special celebration. Everyone buys or makes new clothes for New Year's Day and wears them to Mass on New Year's Eve. They return home, and at midnight everyone, including any young children who can stay awake, goes outside to wish all their neighbors a happy, prosperous new year. Dancing and music, as always, are a part of the celebration.

Birthdays in Honduras are often only celebrated for children. Adults recognize their birthdays and may receive presents, but there is usually no fiesta. Children, on the other hand, get the best party their parents can afford. They will receive presents if their parents have the money. Typically, the whole extended family is invited over for a fiesta. A large *piñata* ("pee-NYAH-tah") is made by the birthday child's mother, grandmother, or aunt. This is a papier-mâché animal filled with little presents and candy made from sugarcane that is hung from a tree just above the child's head. The birthday child is blindfolded and given a stick with which he or she tries to hit the piñata and break it open to let out all the goodies, which are shared with everyone.

RELIGIOUS HOLIDAYS

Hondurans celebrate the Roman Catholic calendar of religious holidays. They also celebrate the Day of Suyapa, the Virgin Mary, who is the patron saint of Honduras, on February 3.

CHRISTMAS December 24, Christmas Eve, is the most important day of the Christmas season for Hondurans but Christmas Day is the national holiday. Some of the Christmas traditions familiar to Christians around the world are also practiced in Honduras. A Christmas tree is put up in the home with the nativity scene next to it. The baby Jesus is covered with a small blanket until Christmas Eve when he is unveiled, representing the birth of Christ.

Everyone attends an important Mass on Christmas Eve. After church, people visit relatives until midnight when everyone goes outside to wish their neighbors a Merry Christmas. Then there is a large feast until early morning. For the majority of Hondurans, there are presents under the Christmas tree, but these are usually presents made for one another, especially for the children.

The birthday girl swings out at the *piñata*.

Cultural fairs are held every year. Tegucigalpa holds an artisan and tourism fair every December, and La Ceiba celebrates Carnaval the third week of every May. Saturday is the biggest day with parades, costumes, music, dance, feasts, and merry-making in the streets. People come from all over Central America and farther to join in these festivities.

THREE KINGS' DAY Epiphany, on January 6, is the day that celebrates the presentation of Christ to the Three Kings or Three Wise Men. Hondurans call Epiphany Three Kings' Day and celebrate it with their own tradition, by acting out the story of Jesus when he was 12 years old and went to Jerusalem alone. In the Bible story, Joseph and Mary were worried and went looking for Jesus. They found him in the temple speaking with the rabbis. In Honduran villages actors playing the parts of Mary and Joseph go around to homes in the neighborhood knocking on doors and asking if anyone has seen young Jesus. Finally, "Mary" and "Joseph" find Jesus in the village church where they ask the famous question: "Where were you?" to which Jesus answers that he is in his Father's house.

HOLY WEEK is an important religious holiday leading up to Easter. The week starts with Palm Sunday. In Honduras, the celebrants act out another Bible story. An actor chosen to act the part of Jesus rides a donkey into town to the church. People lay down palm fronds in front of the donkey to soften the path. Monday, Tuesday, and Wednesday of Holy Week are celebrated by praying in church at the stations of the cross. On Holy Thursday Hondurans once again recreate a story from the Bible, usually in a park. Thirteen people act out the Last Supper of Jesus and the 12 apostles. Hondurans eat a special fish soup on Holy Thursday and Good Friday—no meat is eaten. On Good Friday, Hondurans visit the stations of the cross once again, only this time each station is acted out by people. At night, the actors become immobile to honor the time when Jesus was entombed. Seven children act as angels to accompany Jesus to heaven.

EASTER is celebrated on Sunday with an elaborate Mass and a family feast afterward. Although there are many Western traditions in Honduras, they do not have an Easter bunny who brings chocolate and Easter eggs.

CITY AND VILLAGE FESTIVALS

Every city and village has at least one annual festival that gathers people from all over the department and sometimes even the country to celebrate. At these festivals, dance groups perform the department's traditional dance as well as the ever-popular punta. Marimba music fills the air and people sing along to traditional songs.

Sometimes these annual festivals are secular—the Orange Festival in the department of El Paraíso in southern Honduras is an example. Often annual festivals are religious in nature, usually celebrating the patron saint of the place. At the village of Campa in southwestern Honduras, for example, an annual festival honors the villagers' patron saint, San Matias. People celebrate with traditional Indian dances called the *guancasco* ("goo-ahn-CAS-coh") and the *garrobo* ("gah-ROH-boh").

Above: **Near Trujillo, Garifuna women in festive red march in a festival procession.**

Left: Caramba **musicians provide lively accompaniment for the dancers.**

FOOD

MOST HONDURANS EAT THE SAME FOOD day in and day out unless they are wealthy. In the rural areas, people usually eat only what they can produce themselves. They cannot afford to buy a variety of foods. But they enjoy food so much that feasts are a part of every fiesta.

Urban people generally are better nourished—because they buy what they need, their diet tends to have a better balance of food groups. However, most Hondurans in the cities do not eat well by American standards. They rarely eat meat, and close to payday they may eat very little.

STAPLES

The typical diet of a Honduran is based on corn. It is the most widely planted crop, cheapest in the marketplace, and grown all year round. Women turn corn into tortillas every day. Red beans are the main source of protein. Mixing beans together with corn provides a complete protein. When beans are eaten alone, the body misses out on the essential amino acids that mixing corn with beans provides. People in Honduras and other Central American countries have come to know this, which is why beans and corn tortillas are eaten daily, sometimes at every meal.

White rice is also a staple food. Cassava, another important food, is a tropical plant with a large starchy root. Plantains, which resemble bananas, are used in many recipes.

OTHER TYPICAL FOODS

Most rural families own a cow, and from the milk, the women make *cuajada* ("kwah-HAH-dah"), a kind of cottage cheese that is slightly different from the North American cottage cheese. Most Hondurans do

Above and opposite: **Cassava and corn are two important staples in the Honduran diet, and both are grown year-round.**

Hondurans often eat fruit when they want something sweet. The type of fruit eaten depends on the region. Those who live on the Caribbean coast have the greatest variety. The most popular are bananas, pineapples, mangoes, papayas, and berries.

not drink milk as a beverage but eat the cream, sour cream, and cheese the milk provides. Although almost every rural household raises chickens and pigs, it is a rare treat to have meat. On rare occasions pork is eaten, perhaps as a dish at a feast during a fiesta. Fish is more commonly eaten, especially in coastal towns. Hondurans usually eat their fish fried or in soups and stews.

Fried bananas, a popular snack, are often sold in the marketplace. *Tajaditas* ("tah-jah-DEE-tahs"), or crispy fried banana chips, and sliced green mangoes sprinkled with salt and cumin are sold in bags on the street.

Green vegetables are often missing from the diet, but peppers, especially hot chili peppers, are eaten with many meals. Hondurans, especially the rural poor, also eat a sweet bread. Among the people living on the Caribbean coast, a coconut bread is eaten almost daily.

A Chortí woman makes tortillas in her kitchen.

POPULAR DISHES

Nacatamales ("nah-kah-tah-MAH-les")—large corn cakes stuffed with vegetables and meat—are usually bought in the marketplace or made by those who can afford meat. *Tapado*("tah-PAH-doh"), a dish from the Black Carib, is a stew made with meat or fish, vegetables, and cassava. *Sopa de mondongo* ("SOH-pah de moan-DOAN-goh") is a stew made with chopped tripe, part of a cow's stomach.

Baleada ("bah-lay-AH-dah") is another daily favorite. This is a warm corn or flour tortilla folded over refried beans, crumbled cheese, and sour cream. *Baleadas* are often sold cheaply at markets, street stands, or food shacks. Another favorite street food is *tortillas con quesillo*, two crisp, fried corn tortillas with melted white cheese between them. Fried chicken is also a favorite food.

Honduran food is tasty and sometimes spicy-hot. Hondurans use chili peppers, tomatoes, soy sauce, salt, black pepper, cilantro, cumin, onions, sweet peppers, garlic, and beef or chicken stock cubes as a base for soups.

Filled tortillas and other Honduran snacks are typical fast foods sold on the street and in markets.

Hondurans drink coffee at all times, not only during meals.

DRINKS

Coffee is drunk by Honduran adults with almost every meal but tea is not. *Culey* ("KOO-lee") is a very sweet fruit juice drunk especially by children. *Guifiti* ("gwee-FEE-tee") is a tea-like herbal drink that tickles the taste buds and is drunk to detoxify the body. Sodas and colas are found everywhere today, including a few local flavors like banana. Most Hondurans do not drink unflavored milk but *licuados*, milk blended with fruit, are popular.

It is unusual for Hondurans to drink alcohol with a meal. Alcoholic drinks include *aguardiente* ("ah-gwar-dee-EHN-teh"), translated as "fire water," a homemade liquor that tastes of liquorice, and wine, including *vino de coyol* ("VEE-noh de KO-yohl"), a sparkling wine made from the sap of the coyol palm. There are also four kinds of beer made and consumed in Honduras.

PINEAPPLES

Pineapples have been cultivated in Honduras since pre-Columbian times and have therefore made their way into the Honduran diet. Although pineapples are grown commercially around La Ceiba, many families grow pineapples in their yard or family plot.

Every part of the pineapple can be used, even the outside prickly skin, which makes good pineapple tea or vinegar. One of the most popular ways for Hondurans to preserve vegetables is to pickle them in pineapple vinegar. The fruit is pulped for juice to drink and jam for pies. Pineapple tops are put in a bucket with a little water for a month. If roots appear, they go back to the family plot for planting and start all over again.

KITCHENS

Women almost always do the cooking. It is very rare to find a man cooking in the kitchen.

In rural homes kitchens are usually outdoors. A woman has an adobe and sand oven called a *lorena* ("loh-REH-nah") for baking breads. These ovens have no door and are approximately waist-high. Women burn firewood in them for two hours to get the oven hot enough to bake bread. The dough sits in small pans that are placed into the oven by hand. After 20 minutes the bread is usually done, and the loaves are removed from the oven with a long wooden paddle.

A rural woman will often have a wood-fire stove going as well to fry food or boil stews. People who can afford it will have this stove indoors in a kitchen. But even in the cities, an indoor kitchen is not used by everyone.

Wherever food is sold in Honduras, there is usually a tortilla vendor, for no meal is considered complete without this cornmeal bread.

DAILY MEALS

Every meal is generally eaten at home. Children who have many miles to walk to school will eat a meal provided by the school during the day. Some people in the cities go to restaurants for supper on special occasions.

Meals are seldom eaten around a table. If there is no table, the family sit on chairs around the room. Some families eat outdoors because the space indoors is too small. Those who have television may sit around and watch it while they eat. Otherwise, they eat and talk about their day. Wealthier people have a separate room for dining.

Meals are eaten with spoons, forks, and knives, and tortillas and breads are eaten held in the hand.

Red snapper with rice and beans, fried bananas, and a salad—a typical Honduran meal.

BREAKFAST The morning meal is eaten only after some of the morning chores are done. Breakfast may include a combination of the following: red beans and tortillas, eggs, cheese (often *cuajada*), plantains, salty butter on bread, coffee, and even homemade cereal with milk. Poor Hondurans have coffee with bread for breakfast.

LUNCH is usually more substantial than breakfast and may include meat if the family can afford it. A typical lunch would have white rice with pork, beef, or chicken, a soup made of red beans, fish or chicken, and tortillas. *Culey* is often drunk during lunch.

SUPPER is generally a lighter meal than lunch. It usually includes a soup, red beans, eggs, plantains, butter, and tortillas. Meat is not commonly eaten at this meal, even by those who can afford it. Fried beans with onions eaten with a tortilla is popular.

DESSERT Most Hondurans do not eat dessert because they cannot afford the luxury. Where there is dessert, perhaps at a fiesta, sweet cake and ice cream are favorites. *Dulce de rapadura* ("DOOL-say de rah-pah-DUHR-ah"), a candy made from sugarcane juice, is the most frequently seen Honduran dessert.

FEASTS

For fiestas and town festivals, the meals are not very different from everyday meals. But some of the favorites are made for the community party, such as *nacatamales*. Pork, beef, and chicken are commonly reserved for special occasions.

DULCE DE RAPADURA

Candy in Honduras is *dulce de rapadura*, basically a processed sugar cube made from sugarcane and wrapped in cane leaves or corn husks. *Dulce*, as it is called, is usually made by only one campesino in a given village. Sugarcane stalks are cut down and put through a sugar mill powered by cows attached to horizontal wooden braces. The cows walk in a circle to turn the press, and juice from the sugarcane is squeezed out.

The juice is collected, cooked, and then cooled in wooden molds. There may be as many as 50 large molds in one very large rectangular piece of wood. The end product is sold to other people in the village or taken to a market elsewhere. Aside from being eaten as candy, *dulce* is used to sweeten coffee, make fruit preserves, or to sweeten breads.

SOPA DE MONDONGO

2 cups water	2 onions, sliced
1–2 pounds (¹/₂–1 kg) beef, including tripe	6 cloves garlic, crushed
1 head of cabbage	1 sweet pepper
2 large cassava (any variety)	2 tomatoes
1–2 medium *pataste* ("pah-TAHS-teh"), or substitute with summer squash	1 tablespoon fresh cilantro, chopped
1–2 unripe green bananas	2 teaspoons cumin
1 hot pepper (any variety)	1 tablespoon cornmeal to thicken broth
	salt

Cut beef and all vegetables into bite-size pieces.

Boil water, then add beef, cabbage, cassava, *pataste* (or squash), bananas, hot pepper, onions, and garlic. Simmer for 1 hour, adding more boiling water when necessary to cover ingredients.

Then add sweet pepper, tomatoes, cilantro, and cumin. Mix cornmeal with a little water to make a paste and add this to the stew to thicken it a little.

Simmer for another hour. The end result should be a semithick broth, not a gravy. Season with salt to taste.

Serve in bowls on its own or over steamed rice.

When eating out, most Hondurans will order the plato típico *because it is filling and inexpensive besides being a favorite. It includes a combination of some of the following foods— beans, rice, tortillas, fried bananas, beef or fish, potatoes or cassava, cream, cheese, and a cabbage or tomato salad. Many restaurants in cities or small towns offer a cheap, large, fast meal to workers at lunchtime called* plato del día. *The meals differ from place to place but always include tortillas.*

HONDURAS

BELIZE

0   50   100 Miles
0   50   100   150 Kilometers

Swan

Gulf of Honduras

GUATEMALA

Roatán Island

Guanaja Island

Utila Island

Bay Islands (Islas de la Bahía)

Cayos Cochinos Islands

Trujillo

Puerto Cortés

La Ceiba

Tela

San Pedro Sula

Cordillera Nombre de Dios

Mount Bonito

R. Aguán

Aguán Valley

R. Sico

R. Paulaya

R. Plátano

Biosfera Río Plá

La Lima

El Progreso

Cordillera Merendón

R. Ulúa

El Cajón Reservoir

Yoro

La Unión

Copán

Santa Rosa de Copán

Lake Yojoa

Juticalpa

Mount El Pital

Mount Celaque
(9,350ft / 2,849 m)

Gracias

Siguatepeque

Intibucá

La Paz

Comayagua

Patuca Mountains

R. Patuca

La Esperanza

Marcala

Valle de Angeles

Santa Lucía

TEGUCIGALPA

Cordillera Entre Ríos

R. Coco

Danlí

El Paraíso

EL SALVADOR

N

Nacaome

R. Choluteca

Choluteca

NICARAGUA

Amapala

Gulf of Fonseca

PACIFIC OCEAN

D

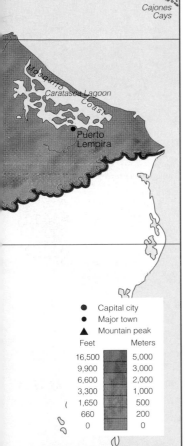

Caribbean Sea

Cajones
Cays

Mosquito Coast

Caratasca Lagoon

Puerto
Lempira

Capital city
Major town
▲ Mountain peak

Feet	Meters
16,500	5,000
9,900	3,000
6,600	2,000
3,300	1,000
1,650	500
660	200
0	0

Danlí, B3

El Cajón Reservoir, B2
El Paraíso, B3
El Pital, Mount, A2
El Progreso, B2
El Salvador, A3

Fonseca, Gulf of, B3

Gracias, A2
Guanaja Island, C1
Guatemala, A2

Honduras, Gulf of, A1

Intibucá, A2

Juticalpa, C2

La Ceiba, B2
La Esperanza, A3
La Lima, A2
La Paz, B2
La Unión, B2

Marcala, B3
Mosquito Coast, D2

Nacaome, B3
Nicaragua, C3

Pacific Ocean, A3
Patuca Mountains, C2
Patuca, Río, C2
Paulaya, Río, C2

Plátano, Río, C2
Puerto Cortés, B1
Puerto Lempira, D2

Roatán Island, B1

San Pedro Sula, A2
Santa Lucía, B3
Santa Rosa de Copán,
  A2
Sico, Río, C2
Siguatepeque, B2
Swan Islands, D1

Tegucigalpa, B3
Tela, B2
Trujillo, C1

Ulúa, Río, A2
Utila Island, B1

Valle de Angeles, B3

Yojoa, Lake, B2
Yoro, B2

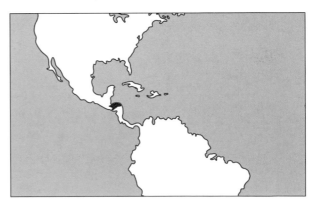

QUICK NOTES

OFFICIAL NAME
Republic of Honduras

LAND AREA
43,277 square miles (112,087 square km)

POPULATION
5.8 million

CAPITAL
Tegucigalpa

MAJOR CITIES
San Pedro Sula, La Ceiba

THE 18 DEPARTMENTS (PROVINCES)
Atlántida, Choluteca, Colón, Comayagua, Copán, Cortés, El Paraíso, Francisco Morazán, Gracias a Dios, Intibucá, Islas de la Bahía (Bay Islands), La Paz, Lempira, Ocotepeque, Olancho, Santa Bárbara, Valle, Yoro

NATIONAL FLAG
Three horizontal bands of blue, white, and blue with five blue five-pointed stars arranged in an X pattern centered in the white band. The stars represent the members of the former United Provinces of Central America: Costa Rica, El Salvador, Guatemala, Honduras, and Nicaragua

NATIONAL FLOWER
The orchid

NATIONAL TREE
The pine

NATIONAL ANIMAL
White-tailed deer

NATIONAL BIRD
The macaw

NATIONAL LANGUAGE
Spanish

MAJOR RELIGION
Roman Catholicism

MAJOR RIVERS
Ulúa, Choluteca, Aguán, Patuca, and Coco

MAJOR LAKE
Lake Yojoa

HIGHEST POINT
Celaque (9,350 feet / 2,849 meters)

CURRENCY
Lempira; 100 centavos in one lempira
13.28 lempiras = US$1

IMPORTANT ANNIVERSARIES
Day of the Americas (April 14)
José Trinidad Cabañas Day (June 9)
Independence Day (September 15)
Francisco Morazán's Birthday (October 3)

MAIN EXPORTS
Bananas, coffee, shrimp, lobster, minerals, beef, lumber

LEADERS IN POLITICS
Francisco Morazán—President of the United Provinces of Central America (1830–39); hero for attempting to unite Central America
José Trinidad Cabañas—past president of Honduras (1852–55); hero of the poor

GLOSSARY

aguardiente ("ah-gwar-dee-EHN-teh")
A local liquor that tastes like licorice

buenos dias ("BWAY-nos DEE-as")
Good day.

campesino ("kahm-pay-SEE-no")
Male peasant.

caramba ("cah-RAHM-bah")
String instrument more often found in rural areas of Honduras.

cuajada ("kwah-HAH-dah")
A Honduran variety of cottage cheese.

culey ("KOO-lee")
A very sweet fruit juice.

duende ("DWEHN-deh")
Fictitious folk character—a short man who lives in the woods.

dulce de rapadura
("DOOL-say de rah-pah-DUHR-ah")
Local candy made from sugarcane and wrapped in cane leaves or corn husks.

evangélicos ("eh-van-HAY-lee-kohs")
Protestant groups.

Ladino ("lah-DEE-noh")
Spanish-speaking people whose lifestyle follows Hispanic patterns.

machismo ("mah-CHEEZ-moh")
Masculine, daring, brave behavior exhibited by men.

marianismo ("mah-ree-ahn-EEZ-moh")
Feminine ideal emphasizing self-sacrifice and loyalty to husband and family.

marimba ("mah-RIM-bah")
Popular, traditional Central American instrument that looks like a xylophone.

mascaro ("mas-KAH-roh")
Mask dance of the Garifuna people.

mestizo ("mes-TEE-zoh")
People who are a racial mix of indigenous (Indian) and European ancestry.

nacatamales ("nah-kah-tah-MAH-les")
Corn cakes stuffed with vegetables and meat.

niño, niña ("NEE-nyo, NEE-nya")
Child.

novena ("noh-VAY-nah")
Nine nights of prayer after a family member's death and on the death anniversary.

piñata ("pee-NYAH-tah")
Colorful papier-mâché figure filled with candy and small toys.

punta ("POOHN-tah")
Traditional dance of the Garifuna, performed after death; today a modern dance in discos.

stations of the cross
Tableaux placed in or outside a church to represent scenes from Christ's life from the Last Supper to his crucifixion. Church members visit the stations of the cross to pray.

BIBLIOGRAPHY

Adams, Richard, N. *Cultural Surveys of Panama, Nicaragua, Guatemala, El Salvador, Honduras.* Detroit: Blain Ethridge 1976.

Barry, Tom. *Central America: Inside Out.* New York: Grove Weidenfeld, 1991.

Benjamin, Medea (translator and editor). *Don't Be Afraid Gringo: A Honduran Woman Speaks From The Heart. The Story of Elvia Alvarado.* New York: Harper and Row, 1987.

Lands and Peoples Vol. 6. Danbury, CN: Grolier Inc. 1993.

May, Charles Paul. *Central America: Lands Seeking Unity.* Toronto: Thomas Nelson and Sons, 1966.

Merrill, Tim L. (editor). *Honduras: A Country Study.* 3rd edition. Federal Research Division. Library of Congress, Headquarters, Dept. of the Army, 1995.

Panet, Jean-Pierre, Leah Hart, Paul Glassman. Updated by Howard Rosenzweig. *Honduras and Bay Islands Guide.* 4th edition. New York: Open Road Publishing, 1997.

Weddle, Ken. *Honduras In Pictures.* 2nd edition. Minneapolis: Lerner Publications, 1994.

INDEX

INDEX

INDEX

PICTURE CREDITS
A.N.A. Press: 50, 56, 57, 77, 113
  (top)
Björn Klingwall: 34, 37, 43, 44, 70,
  72, 101, 104, 119
Jason Lauré: 68 (bottom)
Vicente Murphy: 5, 6, 7, 8, 10, 11, 14,
  15, 16 (bottom), 18, 20, 22, 23, 27,
  28, 30, 35, 40, 42, 45, 52, 53, 54,
  55, 59, 62, 64, 66, 68 (top), 79, 81,
  82, 92, 93, 94, 97, 98, 99, 100, 102,
  106, 108, 110, 113 (bottom), 114,
  115, 116, 118, 123
Chip & Rosa María de la Cueva
  Peterson: 24 (bottom), 33, 65
David Simson: 1, 3, 21, 24 (top), 46,
  47, 48 (bottom), 49, 58, 69, 71, 74,
  76, 78, 83, 84, 86, 89, 90, 95, 105,
  111, 117, 120
South American Pictures: 4, 17, 19,
  25, 26, 36, 48 (top), 51, 60, 63, 85
Graeme Teague: 12, 16 (top), 41, 67,
  73, 103
Topham Picturepoint: 80

The author thanks these
interviewees:
Jessica Leninova Nuñez Moreno
Elda Soraya Martinez Avíla